The
Teacher's
Journey

The
Teacher's
Journey

The Human Dimensions

Jeffrey A. Kottler

Ellen Kottler

CORWIN

A SAGE Company

CORWIN
A SAGE Company

FOR INFORMATION:

Corwin

A SAGE Company

2455 Teller Road

Thousand Oaks, California 91320

www.corwin.com

SAGE Publications Ltd.

1 Oliver's Yard

55 City Road

London, EC1Y 1SP

United Kingdom

SAGE Publications India Pvt. Ltd.

B 1/I 1 Mohan Cooperative Industrial Area

Mathura Road, New Delhi 110 044

India

SAGE Publications Asia-Pacific Pte. Ltd.

3 Church Street

#10–04 Samsung Hub

Singapore 049483

Acquisitions Editor: Jessica Allan

Associate Editor: Julie Nemer

Editorial Assistant: Lisa Whitney

Permissions Editor: Jason Kelley

Project Editor: Veronica Stapleton

Copy Editor: Diane DiMura

Typesetter: Hurix Systems Pvt. Ltd

Proofreader: Talia Greenberg

Indexer: Karen Wiley

Cover Designer: Gail Buschman

Copyright © 2013 by Corwin

Printed in the United States of America.

Library of Congress Cataloging-in-Publication Data

Kottler, Jeffrey A.

The teacher's journey : the human dimensions / Jeffrey A. Kottler, Ellen Kottler.

p. cm.

Includes bibliographical references and index.

ISBN 978-1-4522-1827-4 (pbk.)

1. Teaching. 2. Teachers—Conduct of life. I. Kottler, Ellen. II. Title.

LB1025.3.K668 2013

371.102—dc23

2012024497

This book is printed on acid-free paper.

SUSTAINABLE FORESTRY INITIATIVE

Certified Chain of Custody
Promoting Sustainable Forestry
www.sfiprogram.org
SFI-01268

SFI label applies to text stock

12 13 14 15 16 10 9 8 7 6 5 4 3 2 1

Contents

Acknowledgments

On our journey we have come into contact with many students, teachers, and administrators who have enriched our lives personally and professionally. We appreciate and thank those who have shared their insights with us and inspired us along the way.

We would like to thank Jessica Allan and Paul Smith for their support of this book, along with the dedicated Corwin editorial and production professionals.

About the Authors

Jeffrey A. Kottler, Ph.D., is one of the most prolific authors in the fields of psychology and education, having written eighty books about a wide range of subjects during the past thirty-five years, including textbooks for teachers and counselors; resources for practitioners; and nonfiction bestsellers about interesting phenomena such as true crime *(The Last Victim),* crying *(The Language of Tears),* conflict *(Beyond Blame),* creativity *(Divine Madness),* entertainment violence *(Lust for Blood),* lying *(Duped),* and social justice issues *(Changing People's Lives While Transforming Your Own).* In addition, he has written over a dozen books for teachers, most in collaboration with his wife, Ellen, and published by Corwin.

Jeffrey has worked as a teacher and counselor in a wide range of settings including preschool, middle school, high school, community college, and university. He has served as a Fulbright Scholar and Senior Lecturer in Peru (1980) and Iceland (2000), as well as worked as a teacher in New Zealand, Australia, Hong Kong, Singapore, and Nepal. Jeffrey is professor of counseling at California State University, Fullerton, and president of Empower Nepali Girls (www.EmpowerNepaliGirls.org), which provides educational scholarships for at-risk children in Nepal.

Ellen Kottler, Ed.S., has been a teacher for over thirty years in public and private schools, alternative schools, adult education programs, and universities. She has worked in inner-city schools as well as in suburban and rural settings. She was a curriculum specialist in charge of secondary social studies and law-related education for one of the country's largest school districts. Ellen is the author or coauthor of several books for educators, including *Secrets for Secondary School Teachers: How to Succeed in Your First Year; On Being a Teacher; Secrets for Beginning Elementary School Teachers; Counseling Skills for Teachers; English Language Learners in Your Classroom: Strategies That Work; Secrets to Success for Science Teachers;* and *Students Who Drive You Crazy: Succeeding With Resistant, Unmotivated, and Otherwise Difficult Young People.*

She teaches secondary education and supervises intern teachers at California State University, Fullerton.

1

The Journey of a Teacher

Rewards, Challenges, and Phases

> *Teaching is often referred to as a job, sometimes as a career, or even a profession, but it is far more than that: We consider the choice as a way of life, or even a way of being. The teacher's journey represents a lifelong commitment to learning, not only about your content area, grade level, curricular changes, school policy, and technological innovations, but about true passion for new knowledge and skills that make you more effective as a professional— and a human being.*

It is remarkable when you consider that the teacher's journey is one of adventure. Each year we encounter new students and become a part of their lives, just as they become members of our community. We are witnesses to their joys and their sorrows. We watch as they learn, grow, and mature, as well as when they falter, make mistakes, and fail. We do our best to support, encourage, and inspire them to succeed. With our words, as well as through our actions, we model for them what is possible and what they can achieve. It is certainly through our skills, knowledge, and expertise, but also through our very presence, that we demonstrate our faith in their abilities.

We were working in a school in Southern India. This was in a lower-caste "Dalit" village that had been destroyed by a tsunami a few years earlier, adding even greater burdens to those of the "untouchable" caste that were operating in survival model. In spite of their hardships, the children loved going to school, mostly as an escape from some pretty challenging family situations, often with the father absent trying to earn money as a fisherman or porter, or in some cases, a victim of alcohol abuse.

A group of us, all volunteers, were assigned to various classrooms. I (Jeffrey) ended up teaching kindergarten along with a college student, Monica, who was even more frightened than I was, given the vast cultural differences between us and the students. These were four- and five-year-olds who did not yet speak English, or even Hindi (I understand a bit of Nepali, which is close). Also, given our age differences, I wondered if I still had the stamina to keep up with the little ones; besides teaching college and graduate students, most of my prior school experience has been in secondary settings, although my first teaching job eons ago had been in a preschool. My partner, Monica, was terrified for a different reason in that she had minimal formal training in education and wondered how she would manage the class of rambunctious bundles of energy who were absolutely fascinated by their two white-skinned substitutes.

As it turned out, the children were so incredibly curious and well behaved that it was a dream teaching job. We knew songs and games and activities that were novel for them. We had come equipped with new books, art supplies, and even a Frisbee! Whatever we tried with the children seemed to rivet their attention, although it was difficult to tell what they were thinking most of the time. Most of all, they loved saying our names and having us repeat theirs so they could make fun of our accents.

Here was a twenty-year-old and a sixty-year-old collaborating as coteachers, although as much as possible I took a backseat because Monica was so amazing to watch with the kids. She was a natural in the sense that her love for the children was contagious. Whereas I was focused on following our assigned curriculum, teaching the alphabet, drilling them in numbers, trying to corral them to stay reasonably focused, Monica was all about validating these children who had been so neglected, abused, and impoverished that they couldn't believe that we were even paying attention to them at all.

But here is my most lasting vision of what that experience was all about—and I will remember this until my last dying breath. It was time for us to leave and move on to the next location where we would be volunteering. It had been an amazing experience but also an exhausting one in which I could barely stay on my feet. I ritually said goodbye to each child as they giggled at my mangled pronunciation of their language. I looked across the room and there was a long line of wiggling children standing in front of Monica. If you know anything about Indian culture, much less the culture of five-year-olds, you would realize that, in itself, this was remarkable. And each child was waiting patiently for his or her turn to approach Monica. She bent down and picked up each child in turn and hugged him or her in her own arms, rocking back and forth, planting a kiss on the forehead and showing the most glorious smile. Each child felt bathed in love and seemed to float away, eyes full of tears. I watched the scene unfold trying to stifle a sob in my chest. I was so incredibly moved by the power of Monica's touch and her love that I felt as if I was in the presence of an almost mystical experience. I take that back: It *was* a mystical experience.

Regardless of whether you are a first-year teacher, a new student in the profession, or on the verge of retirement, we are all moved by instances similar to what was just described. We were challenged in ways that tested our resolve and commitment, that pushed us beyond what we knew and understood, beyond what was familiar and comfortable, and yet that provided a sense of fulfillment that bordered on ecstasy.

We all became (or are becoming) teachers in the first place because we want to make a difference in the world. We thrive on learning, not only for ourselves, but also for the students we are privileged to help. In our own modest ways, each of us is changing the world, making it better, one child at a time.

Time for a reality check, lest we get completely carried away: teaching represents the best of times . . . and the worst of times. There are days when we can't believe we actually get paid for our work, given how exciting and fun it is introducing students to new ideas and skills that they can begin to apply immediately. Yet there are other times we want to bang our heads against the wall in frustration, wondering what the heck we are even doing in this godforsaken profession that feels so unappreciated and disrespected.

The teacher's journey is filled with trials and tribulations, just as one would expect during any adventure. Much of the time we feel lost, without an accurate map or working compass. There are obstacles to overcome and adversaries to face, but also exciting and novel experiences. Best of all are the relationships we develop with many of our students, some of their parents, and cherished friends and colleagues.

THE JOYS OF TEACHING

The rewards of teaching are immediate and long-term. We get to hear students speaking a new language we have taught them, playing an instrument they had never held before, and analyzing literature in a book they have read for the first time. We observe students learning to write, multiplying polynomials, baking a cake, or creating an artistic masterpiece, as well as mastering many other objectives. We know, if not for the environments we created and the nurturing we provided, the students would not have these experiences to call their own.

We get to know students' individual differences, abilities, and interests. As mentioned in the previous example in India, our greatest source of joy and satisfaction arises from knowing we have made a difference. We may have not reached all the children in a significant way, or even most of them, but each year it is just enough to sustain us and feed our faith in the power of teaching.

It's exciting (and sometimes frightening) to enter an empty classroom in the morning and never know exactly what will transpire. Each day is novel and different. Each group of students has its own personality. Each hour is unique. Yes, we plan, we gather materials, we know from experience what the likely frustrations will be, but we don't know precisely what the timing will be, when the "ah hah" moments will occur. Our time is never predictable. At the end of the day, when the room is quiet once again, we see remnants of what was on the boards; the initial seating arrangement; the pages in books turned; the computer screens blinking; the used pens, pencils, and other equipment, all evidence of the students' activities. We think about the great variety of people we have interacted with throughout the day—not only the students, but also other faculty, administration, staff, and parents/guardians.

In the classroom, we see students improve in their academics and athletics, but also in the social arena. We bring together students who do not know one another and who do not necessarily know how to get along to develop a community. Throughout the year, we work with them to develop communication skills, helping skills, and leadership skills. At the end of the year, if not sooner, we see the results: students who can collaborate but can also work independently.

As time goes on, former students come back to visit. They notice what is new or that we've rearranged our rooms. They tell us how their lives have changed. They share how what we did made a difference to them.

Sometimes, we have to wait a long time. Recently, I (Ellen) received an e-mail with "Are you Mrs. Kottler?" as the subject heading. My interest was piqued, wondering who was looking for me. Twenty years ago, this particular person (now married with children of her own) was a student in my class and now she wanted me to know that she had been thinking about me and our experiences together. Given that there are many days that I wonder why I still stick with this profession, given my frustrations and challenges, I was elated for days afterward knowing that all the work is sometimes so appreciated.

The tangible rewards of our profession are easy to list: a stable paycheck, benefits, retirement; pay increases based on longevity and education; stable work hours during the week; flexible time in the afternoons, especially to be with our own children; holiday and summer vacation days; and ability to call for a substitute when we are sick. Then there are all the opportunities for us to learn and grow, improving our knowledge base, as well as our skills relating to others.

As time permitted over the years, my (Ellen) "domain" has significantly expanded. Over the years, I have attended so many plays, concerts, recitals, debates, athletic events, competitions, and performances. I have visited students' homes and places of employment. I have toured their neighborhoods and lived in their communities. I have followed them as they went to college or a university, into the military, and then on to various careers. I have watched students' accomplishments with pride, knowing that in some small way I have been part of their journey, a guide along the way.

For some fortunate and passionate professionals, teaching is far more than just a job—it is a calling. For others it's a way to give back to the community. Perhaps a teacher once helped them when they were in need growing up and they want to do the same for others. For others, it's a way to contribute to the future of our society, a civic duty. Regardless of what teaching does to serve others, it does so much to enrich our own lives in a multitude of ways.

TESTS OF COMMITMENT

In spite of all the benefits and joys that accompany a teacher's journey, there are also incredible challenges. The number of new teachers who abandon the profession after a few years is disturbing; as many as one-third within the first few years. We acknowledge there are many obstacles facing teachers today. Some are related to the classroom, others to the system in which teachers work, still others the result of larger societal issues. In some cases, there has been a loss of faith in the system itself. With greater emphasis on test scores, reduced support, and less than ideal working conditions, many teachers feel discouraged and dispirited. Stress is also exacerbated by the "emotional labor" associated with the job in which we often function in a nurturing role, with all the accompanying baggage.

Consider this very brief list of common complaints as a starting point:

- *Disruptive students.* One (or more) annoying, disruptive student seems to take 75 percent of your attention during the day and after school ends! Classroom management is an ongoing task.
- *Extent of assessment.* Administering quizzes, tests, benchmarks, grading, recording, giving feedback are all time-consuming tasks taking away from instruction. Standardized testing has changed curriculum focus and delivery of instruction. It involves teachers as test administrators requiring extra meetings to learn test protocol and duties of counting and delivering test booklets.
- *Unappreciative students.* We care so much and they sometimes seem to care so little. They are much more interested in one another than us.

- *Parents who undermine our efforts.* We spend all day working with children, doing our best to support and encourage them, and then feel helpless when they return home to the dysfunctional families that undermine our efforts.
- *Interruptions of schedule.* The schedule is constantly changing: fire drills, shelter-in-place drills, assemblies, late-start days, snow days, early-out days. There are also shorter calendars due to mandated testing, furlough days, or limited budgets.
- *Unsupportive administrators.* Some principals don't appear to understand the realities of what teachers face, or they have forgotten what it is like to be in the classroom.
- *Demanding curriculum.* The amount of curriculum teachers are expected to cover has increased. We are faced with lists of standards that are virtually impossible to meet.
- *Doing more with less.* There are fewer resources in the classroom, out-of-date textbooks or technology, and increasing class sizes. Music, art, and library programs are cut. Schools are in various states of disrepair as maintenance lists get longer and longer.
- *Toxic colleagues.* We come in contact with faculty who seem mean-spirited, rigid, and controlling, or who just don't seem to care.
- *Remaining current with technology.* We need to constantly update existing software, learn new programs, and add new technology to our repertoire. More and more the emphasis seems to be how we deliver content, rather than the material itself.
- *Social media and mobile technology.* In addition to struggles with our own technology, we must deal with all the distractions related to students' obsession with social media and mobile devices.
- *Staying current with pedagogy.* There are professional development workshops and conferences to attend. Journals and books report on results of recent research in the field.
- *Student values and interests change.* We note how quickly language changes. No longer do students "date"; they "hook up." There is more to keep up with: new music, reality television shows, and apps.
- *Policies and procedures.* The "paperwork" increases. Though we report using computers for efficiency, the number of requests for information increases and we must learn how to submit forms online. New policies are constantly implemented. Then, some policies are unrealistic when applied to individual children.
- *Familiarity of routine.* We see the same undesired behaviors as we teach the same content year after year. Even the pendulum on professional development swings back to where it began, with an emphasis on reading and math. Wait long enough and a software program will become obsolete or the license will not be renewed.

- *Personal economic reality of being unfairly compensated.* We compare ourselves to others whose jobs don't seem as critical and yet they are paid so much more (i.e., business owners, athletes). Recent cuts in health benefits and furloughs have had great impact on our lives.
- *Physical exhaustion.* It is just so draining to be on your feet all day, constantly in motion.
- *We are getting older.* The children never age and we are a year older—every year.

Reviewing this list, or others you might consider, there are many reasons to reconsider one's decision to go into teaching in the first place. It is no wonder that so many in our profession feel overwhelmed and have lost some of their initial passion and enthusiasm. Yet there are ebbs and flows in the development and life cycle of any profession and during any life journey.

LIFE CYCLE OF A CAREER TEACHER

Students aren't the only ones learning in the classroom: One of the gifts of teaching is that we are privileged to learn almost as much as our students. Every day presents opportunities to increase our knowledge, our understanding of the world—to get not only a deeper appreciation of the lives of children, but also a greater understanding of ourselves. The skills that make us effective teachers involve persuasion, explaining things in comprehensible terms, connecting with others in trusting relationships, inspiring people to work harder and reach further. Interestingly, these are the same attributes that make us better friends, family members, partners, and parents. Additional training and experience help us to become more attuned to others' needs and more responsive to them.

There is a developmental progression in most teachers' journeys in which we progress through a series of stages, increasing our abilities and skills along the way, but also facing unique challenges to be negotiated. As in any developmental model, the stages are rather fluid and hardly discrete; it is entirely possible to skip a stage, just as it is likely some people never move beyond a certain level.

Preservice Teacher: "I want to be a teacher when I grow up!"

It is an abrupt change indeed making the transition from "civilian" to a member of the corps of teachers. For many beginners this is the first time you passed over jeans in the closet to make another clothes selection. You are now addressed by title and last name. Students will ask you questions—and expect reasonable answers. Colleagues will look at you and smile in amusement at your naïveté. It's likely you spend hours observing students and teachers, visualizing yourself as the academic leader in the classroom.

You have read about discipline policies, teaching strategies, and assessments. Now it is time for the application. You feel excited, nervous, anxious, eager, but not nearly as ready as you'd prefer.

Student teaching is the time for trying on your professional role, experimenting with what it feels like to *be* a teacher. For years you have entertained fantasies about what it would be like standing in front of your own classroom. Maybe you imagined just how you would arrange the room, how you would present yourself, perhaps even how you would introduce yourself that memorable first day.

You start out slowly, writing your first lesson plans, grading papers, calling parents, taking attendance, completing other tasks as assigned by your master/cooperating teacher or instructor. You begin to teach parts of a lesson, an introduction, body, or closure working your way toward taking responsibility for a whole lesson. You meet your new colleagues and feel in awe of some of their easy self-assurance and the ways they navigate through the school; you see others who just make you shake your head at their inertia or bitterness.

This is a period of trial and error—a variety of errors. Hopefully, you have support and good supervision in place to guide you through reflection because no matter how well prepared you think you are, you feel flooded reviewing all your miscalculations and bungled efforts. You wonder how you can possibly learn all the rules of the school, much less match student faces with names. You have second thoughts about whether you made the right decision to pursue this particular professional path. Yet once the master teacher or university supervisor backs off, you are finally in charge and can't believe the exhilaration you feel. Sometimes you look around and can't believe where you are and what you're doing.

> *I'll never forget my master teacher. I was fortunate to be assigned to someone with so much experience—and so much patience. He first had me observe him in action and then we'd discuss what he did and why. We talked about when and how to use stories in class or when to break students into smaller groups—and how to keep them on task. He was brilliant at bringing himself into the room, sharing parts of himself, yet without seeming self-indulgent. He was human to his students and to me.*
>
> *We were working in a very rural school, in stark contrast to my background from a big city. He taught me so much about getting outside myself to meet the children where they were in terms of culture and context. He was able to do this because he gave me permission to be myself in the room instead of trying to imitate him.*

The New Teacher: "I have keys to my own classroom, but how will I learn their names?"

The next stage in the journey involves the transition from student to beginner. You have prepared for this awesome responsibility, but with a certain amount of trepidation. You put your organizational skills in operation, discovering that things aren't necessarily what you anticipated. Even with the best of intentions and most rigorous planning you soon learn that one of the most important survival skills is the ability to go with the flow, to alter your plans according to the moment.

Each day brings new insights as to how students function, how colleagues get along, what administrators expect, as well as your own strengths and limitations. You become aware of how many decisions and how many adjustments you make throughout the day. You realize how your mood influences others—for better or worse. You learn how to establish routines and pace yourself throughout the day to make it through the week. The good news is you become more efficient in lesson planning, more accurate in timing, more comfortable in your relationships with students. You get to know the climate of the school and make connections in the community. You find the resources that are available to you and your students and enlist the aid of others. You note the progress (including baby steps as well as giant leaps) students are making and gain increasing confidence in your role as a teacher.

But the first year is a difficult one, perhaps one of the toughest of your life. Sometimes you feel like you are in "survival mode," trying to conquer the demands each day presents. Most of the time you feel like you have some idea what you are doing, but you still have reservations regarding whether you can continue to meet the daily expectations of what you sense will be a very long year. You may feel isolated as the only adult in the classroom with precious little time to talk to colleagues during prep periods or breaks. You try not to let others sense your doubts and fears of incompetence. You seem to catch every cold that goes around. The hours devoted to the job are long, as there are so many details to attend to. When the last school bell rings, it seems like it is five o'clock and you haven't even straightened up your desk or erased the board yet.

> *I remember my first year just trying to figure out my way around the school campus. I got lost constantly, not only in terms of finding my way in the building but just keeping my head above water. I'm not so good remembering names during the most ideal situation, but all of a sudden I had all these students who expected me to know who they were, plus all the staff in the school. My head was in a fog.*

On top of that, my students came from backgrounds that were so different from what I was used to. There were all these schedules and activities going on in which everyone seemed to know where they were and where they were going next, everyone but me. All I wanted to do was just stay in my room and catch up on the mountain of grading assignments I had to do. I'd skip lunch altogether or just grab something at my desk. I think other teachers thought I was antisocial or something, but it's just that I was so overwhelmed I had to get my head together during some quiet time.

When I did go to the staff lounge, I'd sit there quietly trying to figure out who were friends with whom. There are all these different cliques and coalitions, and I wanted to stay out of the school politics as much as I could. But that was a mistake, too: I didn't realize at that point how important it was to start networking and building my own support system. It took me another two years before I started to feel really comfortable in my job and gained the confidence to feel like I knew what I was doing.

The Proficient Teacher. "I can't believe I get paid to be with students all day long!"

Sometime between the third and fifth year, most teachers develop a sense of competence and increased confidence. By this point you anticipate what students' behavior will be like and what misconceptions they might bring to the table. You have enough experience to be able to compare student behavior in a broader, normative context. You not only have developed a system to be able to predict and anticipate difficulties, but you've accumulated a repertoire of coping strategies. If your first attempt to deal with a student's crisis, discipline problem, or critical incident doesn't work out, you are prepared to try Plan B, C, or D.

You can sequence instruction in a meaningful way. You are comfortable with the curriculum and have resources to support your teaching strategies. Your assessments give you the information you need about student learning, plus you draw from all the behavior you have observed during the preceding few years. When you feel stuck—which still happens with regularity—you know to whom to turn for help.

You have become more skilled at pacing yourself, realizing you need periodic time-outs to socialize and replenish your energy. In some ways, you may feel a little bored with the routines that have already become entrenched and may yearn to branch out into new areas, take on a new grade level, or teach a different class. You have found opportunities to become actively involved in extracurricular activities in the school, whether in the arena of clubs, sports programs, or service projects. You begin looking for other ways to broaden your horizons and tackle new challenges that will keep you fresh.

It sure is a great feeling to reach that point where I know what I'm doing. I have established a reputation that I'm proud of, that I've worked hard to develop. I've got plenty of friends in the school; in fact, it's interesting how so many of my relationships have changed since I've become a teacher. I prefer to spend time with other teachers because we have so much in common and share so many of the same experiences.

What is most interesting is now how some of the new teachers are seeking me out for advice, just like I was doing just a few years ago. I am by no means an expert, but I do feel like I'm pretty good at what I do. Students trust me. I don't have to prepare so much for my classes now that I have developed the ability to improvise as things unfold. I used to spend hours planning each lesson, each class period; now I just have a basic outline I follow, but I'm fully prepared to go in different directions depending on student interest. If only we didn't have so many of those tests we have to administer I could really have some fun!

I'm also getting to know the families in my school zone. The longer I stay in the district the more I have a second, even a third child from a family. More and more students approach me to show me photos of what they're doing or tell me about what's new in their lives. I especially get a kick out of it when a student calls me "Mom," forgetting for a moment who I am. I prefer to think it's because they find me nurturing.

The Veteran Teacher: "I'm really good at this."

After many years of teaching (or doing anything), you eventually become an expert of your domain, especially if you are reflective about your work and driven to become more effective at what you do. At this stage, you are well aware of the strengths you bring to your job, as well as having learned ways to minimize some of your weaknesses. You know how to motivate even the most reluctant and disengaged students (with varying degrees of success).

With seniority and experience come new opportunities to expand your repertoire. You become more involved in leadership roles, mentoring new teachers, revising the curriculum, advocating on behalf of issues you consider important. You may choose to take on administrative roles, return to a university for further education and advancement, or otherwise keep abreast of new trends through attending conferences or professional development workshops. Perhaps you'll be stimulated to contribute by conducting your own research and writing about it or developing educational resources for other teachers.

With years of experience you also face a new challenge: operating in autopilot. You never want to become like some of the other veterans you've known who appear so burned out with their jobs, waiting out the years until retirement. Your perspective now allows you to see more of the big picture in education. As your own family and social contacts continue to grow, you have also diversified your life so that your job is not as all-encompassing as it once was. Whereas you don't have to work so hard any longer, the timing is perfect because you no longer have the energy you could access in your youth. You've discovered efficient ways to get things done, and you no longer worry so much about the annoying little things that plague beginners.

You have attained a degree of wisdom such that others now see you as a mentor. People come to you more and more often for advice or input. They see you as having power, even though you may not often feel that way yourself. You have reached the pinnacle of your career and it feels good to know what you have accomplished, all the lives you have touched, the generations of students that you have influenced.

> *I think what I enjoy most after all these years is how my school has become a second home. My "teacher friends" are extended family to me. We have shared milestone experiences with each other, some good, some not so good. Together we watch our students grow up and become young adults.*
>
> *I feel so comfortable walking the halls, at ease with all the movement going on around me. Sometimes I just stop and look around, shaking my head at all the things going on at the same time—lockers being slammed shut, kids talking and jostling with one another, everyone in a hurry to get somewhere or do something before the next bell rings. I just take a deep breath and remind myself how lucky I am to be part of this whole scene. I remind myself of all the hard work it took for me to get to this place in my life and career. I know what I do looks easy to others, but they really have no idea what I had to do to feel this way.*

The Waning Teacher: "I know what I am doing."

Teachers in this stage are at the end of their teaching career, whether it was a brief or long tenure. You are very comfortable with what you do and appreciate the rhythm of the year. You know each stage of forming groups in classes will pass. Just as in the beginning of your career, the cycle begins anew: It seems like it takes a lot of energy to get through the day. You notice people ask if you need help carrying things, moving the seats, or picking up supplies; people treat you like you are old even though you still feel like you're thirty (except when you look in the mirror). You may feel less willing to share your extra time with others since you have other priorities going on in your life. You may feel more than happy to leave school as soon as possible at the end of the day to go home and rest, or take care of other things that interest you more. It isn't so much that you are disengaged from school activities as you are content to let the next generation take over. You may not agree with some of their priorities, but you are willing to let them take charge and put your energy elsewhere.

Among all the stages in the teacher's life cycle, this one might be the most diverse in terms of the way it is represented in a given teacher's life. The template just described may not apply at all to some senior teachers who strenuously object to the idea that they are "waning." On the contrary, some teachers don't find their stride until they hit their sixties or later. Rather than feeling on the periphery, they use their experience and wisdom to become even more involved in the profession, not only within the local community but perhaps on a national scale.

> *I think over the years, one thing that I learned that has been most valuable to me is how important it is to remain flexible. My favorite times in the classroom are not when I'm doing something I've done before but rather when my students and I are cocreating some experience I've never imagined before. I love my job most when I depart from my own agenda and move into new territory. I'm frankly bored with my own stories, doing the same things the same way, year after year. No wonder some of my colleagues burn out, since they are basically reliving the same experiences over and over.*
>
> *I've developed a degree of trust in myself, and in the students. I always have a plan, a fairly detailed one at that, that I can adapt in many different ways, depending on the students, their mood, their interests, their readiness. Rather than thinking that every class is the same, I've learned to be more humble and less certain about some things. I try to treat each student, each group, as unique. I look for surprises—and welcome them when they occur—rather than feeling upset when things don't go as expected. I think most of all, the kids teach me so much: They keep my young! I plan to keep teaching until I fall over—or they put me out to pasture.*

The Burned-Out or the Bored-Out Teacher: "Another day, another dollar."

Here is another variation on the theme just described. Despite the efforts to acquaint teachers with the realities of the profession, continued teaching is not a good match for all of us. If teachers don't develop their skills from building relationships to time management to advocating for change, or are not motivated to keep improving, it seems as if the stress overwhelms them or their enthusiasm diminishes significantly. Such teachers may withdraw, refusing to attend meetings; or they may become outspoken, using cynicism as their weapon of choice. They find other reasons to complain, badmouthing everyone to anyone who will listen, including students, parents, other teachers, administrators, superintendents, and the school board. They can't figure out what led them to be a teacher in the beginning of their careers. These teachers become people to avoid, and whereas you might know some who fall into this category, they would never be reading a book such as this; in fact, they stopped reading and learning some time ago.

They put in minimal effort in the classroom and see little achievement as a result. They tend to blame others for their problems and externalize their disappointments: "These kids today—they just don't care"; "It's not my fault they did so poorly since they never study"; "It's not my fault; it's this damn system that's so screwed up." Such individuals feel pessimistic about the future and contemptuous of those who are thriving. They may sense that they are out of date and out of step, but they are tired of change being the constant in their work lives. They resent new innovations in technology or pedagogy, complaining that things aren't nearly as interesting now as they were in the good ole days. Unfortunately, their negative attitudes can become contagious, so they are isolated even further by those in the school who happen to love their work and adore the students.

FINAL REFLECTION

As you reviewed the stages in a teacher's life cycle, you placed yourself in approximate location of where you see yourself in your own career, whether just beginning the journey or in the latter stages. We suspect you wouldn't be reading this book in the first place unless you were hungry for new stimulation, novel ways of conceptualizing your work and its meaning.

There is always a danger in any developmental stage theory to gloss over individual experiences that are so different from what is supposedly normal. Regardless of your own personal rewards from teaching, as well as the particular challenges you face at this time, there are so many opportunities to enrich our professional experiences. While it certainly helps to become exposed to new technology, learn new teaching strategies, master additional content areas, and broaden your knowledge base, we hope to focus more specifically on the human dimensions of our work—the power we hold to inspire others not just by what we know and what we can do, but how we live our lives. It is through our relationships with students that we make the most difference in their lives—as well as feel the most satisfaction from our work.

ACTIVITIES AND APPLICATIONS

1. How did you first decide to become a teacher? This was most likely not a choice that was made in single moment of inspiration but rather a decision that evolved over time—and is continuing to change as you gain more knowledge and experience. Reflect on how your motives have remained fairly stable or have changed over time.

2. Shadow a "master teacher" for a day, not just anyone so identified, but rather a professional who you *know* has extraordinary skills and exceptional talent as a function of her or his vast experience. Observe how this teacher handles the myriad responsibilities that arise during a typical day. Discuss with this person how he or she remains energized and engaged, even after all these years.

3. Consider your current stage of development in the life cycle of a teacher. Compare your own feelings, thoughts, aspirations, and ambitions to those described in the chapter. Use your imagination to project yourself into the future ten years, during which time you will have moved through many of the other stages.

4. It may feel daunting to consider all those things you will learn in the coming years, but it is also true that you have already accomplished so much to get to where you are now. Make an inventory of your achievements about which you feel most proud.

2

Human Dimensions of Teaching

> *Who was the best teacher you ever had? Which mentor immediately stands out as the one who has been most influential and inspirational in your life? This could have been a teacher from elementary school, or high school, or college. It could be a coach or a neighbor or a relative. Whoever it was, he or she was someone who was an absolute master at helping you learn far more than you ever imagined possible.*

Bring to mind a clear image of this remarkable teacher. Hear his or her voice, concentrating not only on its unique resonance and tone but also some special message that still haunts you. Feel the inspiration that still lives within you as a result of your relationship with this teacher. Think about the personal qualities this person exuded that commanded your respect and reverence.

As you recall memories of this individual who was such a powerful model in your life, it is likely that you can identify and list certain personal characteristics that were most memorable. As you review this list of qualities, it may surprise you to realize that very few of these notable attributes have to do with the content of what this teacher taught or even with his or her teaching methods. What is ironic about this phenomenon is that much of teacher preparation continues to be focused on methods courses and in areas of content specialty. The assumption behind this training for elementary and secondary teachers is that when you study a subject in depth and learn the proper methods of instruction, presumably you then become a more competent and outstanding teacher. Not included in this process are a number of other variables that make up the essence of all great educators and infuse them with power—their distinctly human dimensions, including personality traits, attitudes, and relationship skills.

This is not to say that the best educators are not experts in their fields, because they are. Teachers in core academic areas must be licensed by their state, demonstrating that they possess content knowledge through college coursework, examination, or through a process in which the district examines teacher qualifications in terms of subject expertise. But far more than any external certification process, the best teachers know stuff—especially things that interest students the most. Regardless of the grade level and subject matter, excellent teachers are masters of their disciplines.

Yet all the knowledge and skills in the world are virtually useless to those who can't convey their meaning to learners in a personally designed way. Likewise, all the methods crammed into a teacher's bag of tricks are of little help to someone who cannot translate their value in a style that commands others' attention and influences their behavior.

It is the human dimension that gives all teachers, whether in the classroom, the sports arena, or the home, their power as effective influencers. When you review the list of qualities that made your own best teachers effective, you probably noticed that so much of what made a difference in your life was not what they *did* but who they *were* as human beings. They exhibited certain characteristics that helped you to trust them, to believe in them. It didn't matter whether they taught physics or ballet, grammar or bicycle repair, you would sit at their feet and listen, enraptured by the magic they could create with the spoken word and with their actions. They could get you to do things that you never dreamed were possible. It was not so much that you cared deeply about what they were teaching as that you found yourself so intrigued by them as people. You respected them and felt connected to them in some profound way that transcended the content of their instruction. You responded to their example and encouragement. You began to see dimensions of yourself you were previously unaware of—special gifts, skills, ideas. Under their caring instruction, you began to know and value your unique self and find confidence in your personal voice.

NEGLECT OF THE HUMAN DIMENSIONS OF TEACHING

Despite your own personal experiences in being profoundly influenced by mentors and teachers who were eccentric, unique, or otherwise showed a distinctive character, there has been precious little attention directed to this important subject. In a classic handbook for teachers, Arthur Jersild (1955) was among the first of modern-day educators to focus attention on the connection between the teacher's personal life and her or his professional effectiveness. Jersild maintained that understanding yourself is the single most important task in the growth toward developing healthy attitudes of self-acceptance. The basic idea is that to help others, you must be intimately aware of your own strengths and limitations so that you can present yourself in ways that are optimally effective.

The influence of Jersild's little book was short-lived. Soon after it was published, *Sputnik,* the first space vehicle, was launched by the Soviet Union. The United States began a frenzied focus not on teachers' needs, but on the perceived national security imperative to train teachers of scientists and technicians. The human dimensions of teaching were considered too soft to be of great priority.

In the 1960s, during the brief moments of the Great Society and its relevance in education, writers and researchers began to pay more attention to the human aspects of teaching and learning. Carl Rogers, a strong voice for a focus on self in teacher education, wrote extensively about the need for teachers to be process-oriented rather than exclusively content-oriented in their approach. This means spending time in the class discussing not only the poems of Emily Dickinson, the location of national capitals, or the nervous system, but also how children feel about these subjects, about themselves in relation to their learning, and about one another as they continue the dialogue. According to Rogers, teachers must spend considerable time and effort building positive relationships with children, allowing their authenticity, genuineness, and caring to shine through. When these human dimensions are cultivated, a teacher can truly act as an authentic, genuine person rather than as merely the representative of an assigned professional role.

ATTRIBUTES OF A GREAT TEACHER

There may be considerable debate among educational theoreticians and practitioners about the optimal curriculum, the most appropriate philosophy of teaching for today's schools, and the best methods of instruction or discipline, but there is a reasonable consensus about what makes a teacher great, even if these characteristics are uniquely expressed.

Take a minute and reflect on how you ended up where you are right now. What inspired you, or rather *who* inspired you, to consider teaching as a profession? It is likely that you had both negative and positive models—those who struck you as absolutely hopeless as teachers, as well as those who were true masters. If you are like most of us, you entered the profession because one or more of your own teachers had certain attributes that you greatly admired. In fact, you so envied their lives and work that you are now following in their footsteps.

On your personal list—on almost anyone's agenda—is a collection of those human characteristics that are common to the best teachers. These are the attributes that, regardless of a person's subject area, instructional methods, and educational assignment, supply the energy behind a teacher's ability to influence others in constructive ways. The extent to which you have worked to develop these same human dimensions in yourself determines how effective you are as a mentor to others and how satisfied you feel with your choice to be or to continue to be part of this profession.

As we review the personal and professional dimensions of what makes teachers great, we are not so much encouraging you to compare yourself to this ideal as we are suggesting that you take inventory of your personal functioning to assess your own strengths and weaknesses. Such an honest self-examination can help you to identify unexpressed potential that is lying dormant in you— reserves of positive energy just waiting for you to activate them.

There are so many ways that a teacher can capitalize on personal dimensions to help and inspire others. You have known extraordinary instructors who were loud and dramatic and others who were soft and understated. You have known great teachers who were kind and supportive and others who were stern and demanding. You have enjoyed the benefits of working with teachers who were great speakers; others who were captivating one-on-one; and still others who excelled in small, informal groups. You have observed wonderful teachers who may, at first, have seemed to be quite different in their style and personality, yet what they all had in common was that they found ways to maximize their personal strengths. With considerable reflection and some preparation, you have evolved your own style that capitalizes on your strengths and minimizes your weaknesses.

The decision to be a teacher is one with far-reaching consequences. You have committed yourself not only to a lifestyle in which you must become an expert in your field, but also to one in which you have tremendous incentives to be the most well-adjusted, fully functioning, and satisfied human being you can possibly be. What exactly does that involve? Return to your own experiences with the best teachers you ever had. Think again about their personal characteristics that you believe made the most difference to you. Compare these attributes with those that we have listed below. This is not intended to be an exhaustive list, but rather a sampling of what many people mention as most significant. As you review these qualities, consider the extent to which you are working to develop them more in yourself.

Charisma

Since the beginning of human time, those who were tapped for the calling of teacher, whether as priests, professors, or poets, were those who had developed the capacity to inspire others. They emanated a force from their personality that others found attractive, compelling, even seductive in the sense that there was a strong desire to know more about and from them. In the words of the novelist and former teacher Pat Conroy (1982), charisma in teachers occurs when they allow their personality to shine through their subject matter:

> *I developed the Great Teacher Theory late in my freshman year. It was a cornerstone of the theory that great teachers had great personalities and that the greatest teachers had outrageous personalities. I did not like decorum or rectitude in a classroom; I preferred a highly oxygenated atmosphere, a climate of intemperance, rhetoric, and feverish melodrama. And I wanted my teachers to make me smart. (p. 271)*

Scholars may argue as to whether qualities such as charisma are ingrained or can be learned. We would prefer to sidestep that debate and suggest that anyone who has devoted a life to the service of others can increase charismatic powers and thereby command attention in the classroom. This is true whether your inclination is to be dramatic or low key in your presentations, loud or soft-spoken. Charisma, after all, can be displayed in so many different ways, depending on your personal style, not to mention what your students respond best to. It involves gaining access to your own unique assets as a human being, which allows you to find a voice that is authentic, compelling, and captivating.

Randi, for example, is not the kind of person one would ordinarily describe as "magnetic." She is typically quiet and reserved, usually content to hang out on the perimeter of most discussions that take place at parties or in the teachers' lounge. That is not to say that she is not thoughtful and articulate; it is just that she prefers to express herself with restraint, at least when she is around other adults. What most of Randi's friends and family would be surprised to discover is how different she can be behind the closed door of her classroom.

Randi realized long ago that although it is her natural inclination to be somewhat muted, even passive, in her daily interactions, there is no way she could ever control a group of children, much less keep their attention, unless she could learn to gain access to the charismatic part of her personality that she usually kept under wraps. She knew that it was not within her means, or part of her style, to be irreverent, humorous, or dramatic the way some of her colleagues chose to entertain and interest their students. No, the one thing in life that Randi felt passionate about, in her own quiet way, was the beauty and elegance of numbers. As a math teacher, she knew that very few other people (and especially few students) felt the way she did about algebraic equations or geometric theorems. But she believed that if somehow she could communicate to her classes in a natural, authentic way her enthusiasm and excitement about mathematics, maybe some of the energy would become contagious.

Her students would sometimes notice how their usually reserved teacher seemed to come alive at certain times. Her eyes would become electric, her face would become animated. She would start pacing. Her arms would almost vibrate. Her voice would rise not so much in volume as in pitch. She became so caught up in what she was explaining, it was almost impossible not to look at her. Even with little interest in the subject or no understanding of what she was talking about, students could not help but watch her in action. It is so rare, after all, to come in contact with anyone who absolutely loves what he or she is doing and is able to communicate this passion with abandon.

The transformation that would take place in Randi once she was in front of her classes (not all the time, not even most of the time, but enough to keep the students' attention) was, indeed, a form of charisma. She was able to use not so much her compelling personality as her passion for what she was teaching to empower her presentations. Some students could not help but wonder to themselves, "Hey, if this quiet lady can get so worked up over these stupid numbers, maybe there is something there that I'm missing." Others would say to themselves, "I don't much care for this subject, but it sure is fun to watch her in action: It makes me want to learn this stuff."

Charisma, in whatever form it manifests itself, works to command other people's interest in what we are doing. It is not necessary to be an actor or an exhibitionist or to have a florid personality to be charismatic; but it is absolutely crucial to feel passionately about what you are doing and to be able to convey this enthusiasm to others.

Compassion

Children, and for that matter all living creatures, appreciate people who are genuinely caring and loving toward them. This is why the best teachers are so much more than experts in their fields and more than interesting personalities—they are individuals children can trust; they are adults who are perceived as safe and kind and caring. Even when they are in a bad mood, give difficult assignments, or have to teach units that are relatively dry, compassionate teachers will get the benefit of the doubt from students.

When you think again about your greatest teachers, who may not necessarily have seemed like the kindest people, you still had little doubt that they had your best interests at heart. They may have pushed you, may even have shoved you hard, but you knew in your heart that they cared deeply about you as a person. You felt their respect and, yes, sometimes their love.

Very few people go into education in the first place to become rich or famous. On some level, every teacher gets a special thrill out of helping others; unfortunately, after many years in the classroom, some veterans lose the idealism that originally motivated them to be professional helpers. Yet the teachers who flourish, those who are loved by their students and revered by their colleagues, are those who feel tremendous dedication and concern for others—not just because they are paid to do so, but because it is their nature and their ethical responsibility.

We remember vividly the exhilaration that we have felt, and that other teachers describe, when we *know* we have made a difference in someone's life. It can involve explaining an idea that a child has never understood before. It can mean offering a smile, a hug, or a word of encouragement to someone who is suffering. It often involves reaching out in the most ordinary of circumstances to touch someone with our concern and caring. It does not take place only when we are "on duty" in the classroom. Some of the most helpful things that a teacher can ever say to a child take place in more informal settings—in the hallways, on the playground, in the lunchroom—during those times when compassion can be expressed most genuinely.

This compassionate empathy operates not only between parents and children, between therapists and their clients, but also, most assuredly, between teachers and students. It is, in fact, the glue that binds together everything that we do in education. For unless students sense that we really value them and respect them (even as we disapprove strongly of certain ways that they may behave), there is no way that they will ever trust us and open themselves up to hear what we have to say.

You only need to examine your own significant learning experiences to understand the crucial importance that compassion plays in education. Bring to mind, once again, those teachers who have made the most difference in your life, whether a relative, a coach, a professor, a teacher, or whomever. We suggest that beyond the content of what they passed on to you, apart from their formal lessons of instruction, what you appreciated most was what genuinely caring individuals they were. They really cared about your welfare. You trusted them and learned from them because you knew they cared. Actually, that is the foundation of self-esteem; it is based on the regard that others have invested in you. How else can children learn to care about themselves and others if they do not feel such compassion and love from you, their teacher?

If you review what you believe children should receive as a result of their educational experiences, number one on your list (or certainly in the top three) would be developing a sense of self-esteem. It is from this basic attitude toward self that all confidence, competence, and life satisfaction emanate, not only during the school years but throughout a lifetime.

What is it that fosters self-esteem in children? What is it that helps young people to feel better about themselves? Among several other variables, such as mastering age-appropriate developmental tasks, developing competence in life skills, and belonging to a supportive peer group, is receiving lots of support and caring from adult mentors. It is from this position of dedicated, consistent, and compassionate caring that the effective teacher is able to set limits, create and enforce rules, establish effective classroom routines, provide discipline when it is needed—and be able to do so without risk of losing children's respect in the process.

Egalitarianism

Good teachers are certainly not mushy pushovers. Yes, they are compassionate, sometimes even permissive, but they recognize that children need and even crave having the teacher set limits, especially those that are enforced consistently. It is not so much that students despise discipline in the classroom, but rather that they will not abide rules that are unfair or that are applied indiscriminately. It is even safe to say that what children complain about the most in school are those teachers whom they perceive as biased or inequitable in the ways they enforce rules. As one ten-year-old describes her least favorite teacher,

> *She is just so mean I hate her. You never know what to expect. There is this one girl who can get away with anything. She whispers or passes notes and the teacher just tells her to "please be quiet." But if the other kids in the class are caught doing the same thing, then she punishes them. The other day she wouldn't let anybody go outside for recess just because a few kids were causing trouble. I wasn't even talking, but I had to stay inside, too. I just hate her.*

If we consider modeling human qualities to be an important part of the teacher's role, then certainly demonstrating our own sense of fairness is crucial to helping children develop their moral thinking. We cannot forget that teaching is an intrinsically moral act. How are children supposed to learn such values as treating others with respect and fairness unless they see their teachers practicing these behaviors on a daily basis?

Imagine, for example, a situation in which no matter what the teacher does on a particular day, the class is unruly and unresponsive. Cajoling, pleading, threatening, yelling, reasoning, distracting are all met with stony student resistance. The teacher knows that some decisive action is indicated, but for the life of him, he cannot think of what it might be. As he reflects on the choices available to him, he considers the following options:

1. Pick out the ringleaders of the class disturbances and administer after-school detention.

2. Announce to the class that all members are responsible not only for their

own behavior but also for that of their peers. Unless the disturbances cease immediately, *they* will all suffer the same consequences regardless of their relative contributions to the problem.

3. Select the few members of the class who have been seen engaging in the disruptive behavior and subject them to some form of punishment.

As is so often true in any of the behavioral sciences, determining the best and fairest solution to this problem is a judgment call. There is probably no way to predict with certainty that any of the above options is the right one, and that the others are assuredly wrong.

What is at issue here for the egalitarian teacher is not so much what he or she does, but the particular way in which it is accomplished. During the moment of decision, when the teacher is immersed in the fray of classroom conflict, when confusion and frustration prevail, there is simply no time to reason through what will definitely work and what probably will not. Much of the time, the teacher is acting on instinct and experience.

It is not only unreasonable, but even impossible, for students to expect that any teacher will demonstrate perfect equity in all situations and circumstances. What children (and all of us) appreciate is the effort on the part of authority figures to do their best to understand what is going on and try to resolve the conflict with relative impartiality and objectivity. For example, after a heated exchange or conflict, the teacher has an excellent opportunity to discuss with students the process of what took place, how things got out of control, and how situations could be handled differently in the future (such reflective thinking is discussed further in a later chapter). The egalitarian teacher is not necessarily unbiased and just all of the time but strives to be as fair as humanly possible in situations that are often impossible. Where rules are necessary, the egalitarian teaches the rules rather than simply dictates them; even more powerfully, the teacher *lives* the rules by the way he or she behaves in class and daily life.

Appreciation and Responsiveness to Differentness

As we've heard often enough, teachers must address the differences in the diverse abilities and backgrounds of the students in their classrooms. Children with special needs require modifications of curriculum and adaptations in the classroom in order to be successful. For example, a teacher may have a student with a physical disability, a sensory impairment, learning disability, attention deficit disorder, English as second (or third) language, or emotional disturbances, each requiring special attention. Gender and cultural differences also play a significant role in learning styles. There will be different academic and behavioral expectations for some of these students according to an Individualized Education Plan (IEP). The abilities of gifted and talented students present another set of challenges that must be negotiated.

Some teachers treat the challenges inherent in a diverse student population as obstacles to deal with, annoyances that makes the job much more difficult. Wouldn't life be much easier if everyone was exactly the same, from the same homogeneous upbringing, functioning at the same level of ability? Yet other teachers find the diversity in skills, interests, and student background to be enriching for the classroom environment, more realistically reflecting the world at large in which students will be expected to interact with people from all sorts of backgrounds.

Effective teachers will implement different strategies, groupings, and assessments so that each student can be successful. They differentiate the curriculum, the learning activities, and how student progress will be measured. Students may access material through different means and learning styles, such as listening to a CD or podcast, watching a video, chatting online, reading text, or using interactive games. They may work individually, with a partner, in a small group, or as a whole class. Finally, they may be assessed through a traditional instrument or through a form of alternative assessment, such as a product or performance. In this way, students have multiple access points to the curriculum ensuring equity and a variety of ways to demonstrate what they have learned. Students recognize they are all treated fairly, although not the same.

Sense of Humor

If there is one major premise of effective teaching, it is conveying the idea that learning is fun. When students are bored or uninterested, when their attention is diverted toward internal fantasies or external distractions, little learning takes place. In the marketplace of life, we are competing with a variety of other stimuli that are vying for children's attention. While sitting in the classroom, a student may be distracted by unbridled pangs of hunger, longing for peer acceptance, or lust. Compared to the worries, heartbreaks, and interests in their lives, the absolute last thing in the world that many students care about is what you are doing in class. Think about it: Just how important do *you* think what you are teaching is when a child is upset about his parents fighting, or is distraught because a best friend was mean, or is worried about getting a part in the school play, or is excited about an upcoming tennis match?

One principle that is crucial to keep in mind, maybe the single most important concept of education, is that nothing that is taking place in the classroom is as important to children as what they are constructing inside their own internal worlds. Ask a child, any child, how he or she would prefer spending time, and it is likely you will get a long list of possibilities—riding bikes, talking to friends, skateboarding, eating ice cream, playing games, watching television, going to the beach, sleeping late—but quite far down on the list would be the choice, "If I could be doing anything right now, I would like to be in school, right here in *your* class."

It is our job, therefore, not only to teach children, but first to interest them in learning. A sense of humor and playfulness are among the most powerful tools available to teachers to help accomplish this mission. It is one of the ways teachers can connect with students. Play, after all, is the language of children. It is through laughter that we all feel most enraptured, most alive, most connected to what is happening around us.

One of the most challenging teaching assignments that I (Jeffrey) ever faced included a group of preschoolers, ages three to four years. From the looks of their behavior, they did not appear to know the first thing about such ideas as cooperation, sharing, taking turns, or being considerate about others' feelings. I was informed that it was my job to teach them basic social skills (in addition to such life skills as mastering the use of scissors). The hardest part of my task, I soon discovered, was simply commanding their attention for long enough to teach them anything.

None of the usual things I had tried worked very well. I tried being polite—they ignored me. I switched to being unduly firm—they became afraid of me. Yet the one thing these little people taught me that I have never forgotten is that if I could get them to laugh, they would follow me anywhere. I became so unpredictably silly in their minds, prone to do almost anything at any moment, that they were afraid if they turned their attention away for very long, they might miss something really good.

Many children are deprived of the sleep they need to function attentively at school. They may have stayed up watching television, playing video games, or communicating through the Internet. They may have maintained an all-night vigil over a sick or dying pet. They may have lain awake all night as their parents battled and quarreled. They may have been up to finish a project due that day. Whatever the cause, it is every teacher's nightmare—to have to capture the attention of students who are undergoing sleep deprivation. Yet this is the training ground for making superlative instructors. If you can keep these people awake, much less teach them anything, you are indeed in the ranks of the best.

We are not suggesting that teaching and learning are as simple as fun and games. What valuing humor means for the teacher, however, is making a commitment to appreciating the sublime, silly, playful aspects of life. It means spending as much time and attention trying to be interesting and relevant to students' needs as it does preparing the content of what we have to teach. It means acknowledging what is funny and that funny things happen in the classroom. We're sure you already learned the lesson that if you don't encourage play and humor in the classroom, a mischievous student will certainly rise to the occasion and do it for you.

Of the personal dimensions of teaching, humor is the most human of all. Teachers who value humor, who not only tolerate laughter and fun in their classrooms but even invite them in and encourage them to stay, are perceived by students as being more interesting and relevant than those who appear grim and humorless. A sense of humor encourages a teacher to take advantage of those teachable moments that serendipitously come to all classrooms. Your sense of humor will communicate to your students that you are creative, witty, subtle, and fun-loving. Who else would students pay attention to and respect?

Additional Desirable Traits

The best teachers access not just what is in their heads but also what is in their hearts. They are both logical and intuitive. They are responsive both to what they observe on the outside and to what they sense on the inside. In the words of Parker Palmer (2007),

> *We teach who we are: I am a teacher at heart, and there are moments in the classroom when I can hardly hold the job. When my students and I discover uncharted territory to explore, when the pathway out of a thicket opens up before us, when our experience is illuminated by the lightning-life of the mind—then teaching is the finest work I know. (p. 1)*

When adults are asked to reflect on their experiences in school and describe the characteristics of their very best teachers, they mention certain consistent characteristics that impacted them most positively. As you go through this list, think about where you stand in each of these human dimensions:

- *Smarts.* This means you know stuff. You understand things that children want to know. You are perceived as being intelligent not just in "book smarts" but also in "street smarts." You are respected because of your wisdom. Children gravitate toward you because they believe that you know things that are important.
- *Creativity.* You keep students on their toes. You are unpredictable at times, playful and spontaneous. You are able to demonstrate in your own life the sort of creative spirit that you want your students to develop. Rather than overemphasizing "right" answers, you are also interested in promoting their creative behavior, especially the sort that is not disruptive and is "on task."

- *Honesty.* You can be trusted. You are not afraid to say, "I don't know," or "I'm wrong," or "I made a mistake." You model the sort of openness, transparency, and authenticity that encourage others to do the same.

- *Emotional stability.* You are relatively calm. You are not prone to the sort of mood swings or temper tantrums that make children fearful. During those times you become upset, you are able to restrain yourself so you do not lash out at kids. When you do lose control, you do what you can to make things right. You apologize. You accept responsibility for your lapse. You do not blame others. You get help for yourself. Most important, you learn from the experience so you do not do it again.

- *Patience.* Some of the worst teachers are those who are instructing in subjects that came very easily to them. It all seems so simple, and they cannot understand why others have so much trouble. Likewise, when you personally have struggled mightily to master a subject, you can more easily appreciate what others are going through. Patience often comes from this empathic understanding of what is involved in tackling what is perceived as a difficult subject. Time and time again, students mention how important it is for their teachers to be patient with them. We cannot emphasize enough the importance of increasing "wait time" before calling on a student for an answer, of giving students a pause to reflect on what they have learned, and granting them time to make mistakes from which they can progress.

- *Ability to challenge and motivate.* This is a complex characteristic since, on the one hand, you want to motivate students to go as far as they can, but on the other hand, you do not want to overwhelm or discourage them. If you are perceived as having both high standards and a certain flexibility, students will work hard for you, knowing that you will not compare them to others but consider their unique backgrounds and capabilities.

- *Novelty.* Almost everyone enjoys learning experiences that are not the same as what they are used to, within certain limits. Memorable teachers seem to be those who had certain eccentricities, unique qualities, and personal idiosyncrasies that were perceived as "endearing" rather than "annoying." They also try different instructional strategies and are not afraid to take reasonable risks with new approaches.

- *Interest in students.* The revered teachers are the ones who show a genuine interest in their students. They show their school spirit by wearing school colors and participating in school events, attending assemblies, and participating in fund-raising. They engage their students in conversations about their lives outside of school. They not only talk about forthcoming school and community events, they attend concerts, the spring play, debates, sports events, and dances. They meet students at the door and compliment them on their extra-curricular achievements. They are available before and after school to help students with homework for any class, talk about future oppor-tunities, and just listen to what is on their minds. They draw students' interests into their lessons by showing not only that they have heard what has been said, but that is was relevant and meaningful.

In summary, the best teachers have certain qualities that most of us would agree are critical. These include the ability and willingness to do the following:

➤ Know their students well and take a personal interest in them beyond the call of duty
➤ Set high expectations for themselves—and their students, but also goals that are achievable
➤ Make learning personally relevant and fun
➤ Demonstrate humility in the sense that they are always open to new learning—from their students as much as colleagues and written resources
➤ Feel and show a deep passion for what they do that comes across in their excitement and enthusiasm
➤ Be accessible and approachable, with high-level interpersonal skills, sensitivity, and caring

BECOMING MORE PERSONALLY EFFECTIVE

The paradox of being a great teacher is that one must be perceived not only as someone who is playful but also as someone who is efficient enough to get the job done. The job is the business of learning, which if done properly has its own intrinsic rewards. Everyone enjoys the thrill of mastering a new skill or understanding a new concept.

For teachers to be effective in the classroom, as in the world outside of school, it is necessary for them to work at being reasonably well-adjusted human beings. Teachers who are ineffectual or wimpy or whiny, or who are perceived as weak and ineffective in their basic style of interaction, earn little respect from students or from their peers. Likewise, those teachers who appear to be in charge of their own lives, who radiate power, tranquility, and grace in their actions, are going to command attention and respect. Their students will follow them anywhere.

What we are saying is that you have not only the option but the impera-tive to develop the human dimensions of your personal functioning, as well as your professional skills. Teachers are, after all, professional communicators. We relate to others for a living. We introduce people to new ideas. We help students to build their self-esteem and confidence. We develop relationships with people to influence them in positive ways. How are we ever going to do these things unless the children we teach are attracted to us and like us as human beings?

The best teachers are those who have worked hard both to develop themselves as experts in their fields and to practice what they know and understand in their own personal lives. They are relatively free of negative emotions, and when they do become upset they have the skills to regain control. Perhaps most of all, such teachers attempt to live the ideals that they espouse to others. If they preach to others the importance of truth, honesty, self-discipline, knowledge, growth, and taking constructive risks, then they must practice these same values in their own lives. They become living examples for their students, showing that what they say is important enough for them to apply to their own lives. They are attractive models who advertise, by their very being, that learning does produce wondrous results.

Perhaps there are other attributes that you consider to be even more important than the teacher qualities we have identified in this chapter. These may be character traits, skills, values, cultural beliefs, or knowledge that you consider absolutely crucial to teachers who plan on making a difference in children's lives. Whatever choices you would select as being among your highest priorities to develop in yourself, the goal must remain to make yourself not only an accomplished professional but also the most effective human being you can be.

ACTIVITIES AND APPLICATIONS

1. Interview a variety of students representing different grade levels, personalities, and interests. Construct a few questions that seem most intriguing to you, perhaps asking them to identify what they like best and least about their teachers, what annoys them the most, and what they struggle with most consistently. Ask them for advice about what they think would make an exceptional teacher. After you've conducted your interviews, identify common themes that seem most useful. Summarize the list and keep it close to you.

2. Conduct an honest and critical inventory of your own strengths and weaknesses, compared to what you learned from your interviews with students. Select a few of the areas that you most want to improve during the next few years, concentrating on those that seem most important. For example, perhaps students mentioned that what matters

most to them are teachers who truly care about them, and you feel like interpersonal warmth and sensitivity have not been your greatest assets. Make a commitment to get some help where you need it.

3. Invite a trusted colleague to observe you teach with a focus on the more *human* dimensions of teaching. Make sure this friend is someone who will be completely honest with you but provide feedback in a caring and sensitive way so that you feel grateful rather than defensive. Ask this person to focus less on what you *do* in terms of teaching behavior (that's for another time), and more on how you present yourself as a kind, respectful, charismatic, and interesting human being.

4. Observe a few exceptional teachers to observe the ways they use their unique style and personality to create rapport with their students. Notice, as well, how they focus on *process* as much as *content* in the classroom. Reflect on how you might adapt and apply what you have witnessed in the development of your own identity as a teacher.

3

Obstacles and Enhancements to Learning

> *Those special teachers we know, with all the personal and professional qualities we admire, share another important feature that ensures their success: They possess very clear beliefs about learning. They have an understanding about how best to customize content to fit the unique requirements of a situation and the capabilities of students. They are aware of the many obstacles to learning and know how to prevent potential problems before they occur. They know what learning is all about because they are committed, lifelong learners themselves.*

LEARNING VERSUS SCHOOLING

Too frequently much of the professional training and practice of teachers is focused on schooling. Practitioners spend large amounts of time designing lessons; preparing displays; responding to e-mail; returning phone calls; copying materials for students; setting up and enforcing classroom rules; preparing and administering examinations; reporting absences; and readying students for photographs, assemblies, fire drills, recesses, open houses, and hall duty. In their classrooms, students likewise spend inordinate amounts of time copying agendas; completing worksheets; reviewing assignments; doing homework; answering the questions at the end of a chapter; and taking tests, lots of tests—achievement tests, placement tests, pretests, posttests, pop quizzes, benchmark assessments, midterms, and final exams. In the frenzy of these fast-paced and time-consuming activities, a critical distinction is often overlooked. How much of what occurs in school classrooms produces meaningful learning? How much is genuine learning, and how much is just schooling?

Schooling is a compulsory experience in which students are expected to acquire the knowledge and skills of the required curriculum. Schooling demands that students pay attention, listen carefully, take notes, raise their hands to ask pertinent questions, and pass the test at the end of the unit. Schooling requires students to decipher classroom rules, consequences, and routines, which may vary greatly from grade level to grade level, period to period.

Eldridge Cleaver, an African American activist of the 1960s, is a graphic example of the turned-off learner. He spent many frustrating years in class-rooms before he was locked up in San Quentin State Prison for his violations of the law. Cleaver may have acquired the expected spelling and handwriting skills during his years of formal schooling, but he did not learn to make decisions, solve problems, and express his innermost thoughts and feelings in writing. It took the forced confinement of prison before his private voice was liberated. Locked securely behind prison bars, without the aid of teachers or textbooks, Cleaver taught himself to write in order to save himself.

Cleaver's experience demonstrates the critical difference between schooling and *learning*. Schooling is an "outside-in" experience. It is a necessary part of a student's education. Schooling taught him how to follow rules, take turns, play safely, and interact respectfully with teachers and peers. Learning, however, is an "inside-out" process, in which students construct an understanding of themselves, their beliefs and values, and the world in which they live. Learning is a challenging process of discovery that requires little external push; the motivation comes from within. It is the personal quest for new information, new meanings, new challenges and experiences.

Teachers may spend too much time teaching children to follow rules and not enough on actual learning so that we are training the next generation to be followers rather than original thinkers:

"Raise your hand if you have something to say."

"Your reports should be four pages long."

"Make sure you color between the lines."

"Mark your answers by penciling in the circle next to your choice."

"You must sharpen your pencil and be in your seat before the bell rings."

"Don't do anything disruptive—that includes fidgeting, drumming your pencil on the desk, chewing gum, throwing paper in the wastebasket, making noises, or asking questions while I am speaking."

"No talking to your neighbor. If you have something important to say, wait until *after* class is over."

Rules are certainly important for giving students guidelines for monitoring their own behaviors and for understanding the consequences of their choices. Classroom routines and procedures are also necessary for maintaining some degree of organization and order in the classroom. Chaos is no more a constructive environment for learning than is regimentation. But when the focus of teaching becomes classroom management rather than enlightenment, something is out of kilter. Many an experienced teacher would be among the first to complain, "I would love to spend time teaching instead of trying to control these children, but they have no respect for other people. They don't care about school. All they want to do is mess around; they don't want to work."

Well, of course they want to play! Who doesn't? But who said that learning always has to be work, that it cannot be fun? One definition of work is that it is something that you *have* to do, whereas play is something that you *want* to do. Consider, for example, two children who are asked to police the playground for litter. The first child thinks to himself, "What a pain! Why do I always get stuck with these chores? What is this, a prison camp? I hate doing this." The second child talks to herself quite differently: "This is great. I get time to be outside and by myself. Plus, I get to do something important and help make this place cleaner. I love making up stories about how each article I find—a gum wrapper, a can, a shoelace, or a cigarette butt—ended up on the ground where I found it."

The two children are completing the exact same task, yet one views the assignment as the ultimate exercise in frustration, whereas the other treats it as a fun game that gives her an opportunity to relax and use her imagination while accomplishing something worthwhile. If you accept this distinction that your attitude about what you are doing is more important than the actual activity, then you should be spending a whole lot more time trying to foster positive attitudes toward school and making learning fun. This means that learning is so much more than introducing facts or presenting material. It is primarily an internal activity in which a person feels motivated to acquire new and relevant information and skills and, most important, enjoys the process. It is fun, not work, because the learner has reasons for mastering what is being presented.

How do you help children to *want* to learn? How do you encourage them to treat school as fun rather than work? The answer to these questions is simpler than you may imagine. Fun takes place during the following circumstances:

- When you are concentrating with all your effort and energy on a task that you have recently mastered (yes, that does sound suspiciously like work; the main difference is the feeling of competence in accomplishing something that you perceive to be important)

- When you are being challenged to do something that is not beyond your ability and, when mastered, will allow you to accomplish other things that you want to do
- When time flies because you are engaged, doing something interesting and entertaining
- When you are talking to yourself and others about things that are relevant to your life
- When you are interacting with *your* peers and feel understood and accepted by them

We hope that you can see the pattern emerging here. Furthermore, students love learning when the teacher makes an effort to involve them in the process of choosing what they learn about and the way in which they learn it, and when they are helped to personalize the subject in such a way that it seems useful and important to getting them what they want in life.

Window Into a Classroom

Kristen is a substitute teacher. She walks into a new classroom with fear running through her arteries. She has heard about this group of children. They are unruly and disrespectful. Their regular teacher has done nothing but complain about the problems she has encountered: kids coming in late, falling asleep, talking constantly, making obscene noises, generally being downright cruel to one another and to her. Needless to say, Kristen is more than a bit apprehensive. As she enters the room, there is a brief moment of silence as the students stare momentarily at the newcomer before they return to their arguments. Kristen is determined that not only is she going to get them to settle down, but she also is going to make sure they learn something today. Maybe those two goals are related, she reminds herself.

With a confident voice, Kristen introduces herself to this notorious collection of seventh-grade boys and girls: "Good morning, class. My name is Ms. Templeton, and I am here today to share something with you that I think you'll find useful and interesting."

"No, we won't!" a belligerent adolescent male bellows, knowing that he can get away with almost anything with a substitute teacher.

"Yeah? You sound pretty sure of yourself," she challenges the boy. "How can you be so certain that you won't find this interesting? I had no idea you could predict the future."

The class starts to laugh, but it is a nervous, hesitant reaction, as if students are unsure whose side they are on.

"Because we never get to do anything fun in this class," the boy yells back, looking around him to make sure that others are still in support. "Besides," he offers as an afterthought, "social studies is dumb!"

"What could make social studies fun for you?" Kristen asks, mostly stalling for time until she can locate his name on the teacher's seating chart. She finds the name "Amy" listed and realizes that they are playing the "switching names and seats" game.

"Let's talk about the stuff we're really interested in instead of the teacher always talking at us," continues the disgruntled youth in Amy's seat.

"You must be a mind reader after all," Kristen quickly replies, "because that's exactly what I have planned for you today!"

Kristen moves so quickly in having the students rearrange the desks into six groups of five students that they do not have time to level any further protests. She then shares a brief story about teenage friends, Heather and Tina, who spend time together in and out of school. One day, Tina discovers that she has a problem. Her trusted friend, Heather, has cheated her out of some of her hard-earned money and has used it to buy a new pair of sunglasses.

Kristen gives each group fifteen minutes to come up with a solution to Tina's problem. The room begins to buzz as the members of the groups discuss the problem and suggest solutions. From time to time, one of the groups erupts with laughter about one of its off-the-wall suggested solutions. Kristen is surprised to observe that these explosions of laughter do not interfere with the group's ability to complete the task. In fact, the spontaneous laughter appears to help the students deal with difficult decisions and differences of opinion. She gives the groups a warning that they have five minutes left to come up with a solution to share with the whole class.

"Time is up. Move your desks back where they were so we can share our solutions to Tina's problem . . . and class . . . this time I want you to sit in your assigned seats." They smile in recognition that they have been found out.

The remainder of the class period is spent in an animated sharing and comparing of solutions. After each group reveals its unique solution, embellished in an imaginative teenage way, Kristen skillfully leads the students to consider the consequences of their proposed ideas and to reconsider the appropriateness of their original solution. Suddenly, the bell rings, surprising the students who had lost themselves in this interesting class. As they file out, the belligerent male student furtively passes Kristen a note written on a corner of a piece of notebook paper. It says, "Your class was fun. I have a brother who cheats me all the time. I got some ideas today about how to make him stop messing with me. Thanks."

This "window into a classroom" demonstrates one way that learning can be fun, interesting, amusing, punctuated with laughter, and still reach its intended outcomes. An overemphasis on schooling, however, frequently results in students who either become teacher-pleasers, passively going through the motions, or become turned off, frustrated learners often labeled with some learning disability.

Both kinds of students frequently find themselves managed by teachers in classrooms with more worksheets and quiet assignments of "read the chapter and answer the ten questions at the end." Is it surprising that many students find this type of schooling an abysmal waste of their time?

HOW PEOPLE LEARN

In your own schooling experience, you were forced to study theories and concepts related to how children learn and then tested on the material, which may or may not have been presented in a meaningful, practical way. You learned about different approaches to learning, particular ideologies with different names like *constructivist, cognitive, behavioral, humanistic,* and so on. You also may have experienced a fair degree of confusion, as each theory seemed to contradict the others.

In spite of their significant differences, most approaches to learning take into consideration several variables. As a summary, there are certain factors that are most often associated with how learning occurs, especially the kind that sticks with students over time:

- The teaching relationship and the connections you are able to create with students such that they feel valued and respected
- The cognitive activity that takes place internally in which students personalize content in light of their language, background, culture, and experience
- The consequences and reinforcements of behaviors that are rewarded and others that are punished
- The opportunities for practicing and rehearsing new skills and behaviors, with constructive feedback to improve performance
- Cooperative and interactive experiences that allow students to work together to solve problems and apply what is being learned as well as to express their ideas
- Challenges to their current perspective or functioning that force students to develop alternative points of view or strategies
- Introduction to novel ideas and stimulating, enriched environments
- Modeling of effective behaviors

Although hardly exhaustive, this list reviews some of the relatively generic variables that are often associated with constructive learning processes. The more you observe students as they question, examine, explore, and analyze their world, the more you have discovered ways to develop your own methods to encourage their meaning-making efforts.

Learning Styles

Along with learning theories, you have also been introduced to the importance of "learning styles," the unique and preferential ways that each individual acquires and holds on to new skills and information. Learning styles have been classified in innumerable ways, with multiple systems, all of which basically recognize that students learn best when there is a solid match between what is presented, how it is presented, and how the learner relates to the experience. A brief overview of four learning styles is presented below:

- *Sensory modalities*. Visual learners gain knowledge best by seeing new information; auditory learners take in new information best by hearing it; kinesthetic learners like to touch and manipulate objects. While it takes time to gather and develop resources, a teacher who uses pictures, charts, graphic organizers, and text as well as video, direct instruction, and verbal descriptions, along with artifacts, models, and acting out concepts would, indeed, provide a sensory-rich environment for students.
- *Global/analytic information processing*. Global learners move from an understanding of the whole to the contributions of the parts, focusing on spatial and relational processing; analytic learners move from the parts to the whole, using details to build understanding. While students use both types of processing, they typically have a preference of one over the other. Strategies for teachers include modeling and providing practice experiences for students in both types of processing.
- *Field-independent/field-dependent*. Field-independent students prefer to work alone and receive recognition for their individual endeavors; field-dependent students like to work with others and look to the teacher for direction. To address both domains, teachers need to offer both self-directed, individual projects and collaborative, cooperative activities.
- *Impulsive/reflective*. Impulsive students are quick to give responses without much thinking, often guessing at answers; reflective students take their time before replying. Teachers need to provide opportunities for students both to make on-the-spot predictions and to wait before calling out an answer so as to give all children a chance to formulate a response.

Additional theoretical models emphasize the idea of "multiple intelligences" rather than learning styles, but the basic concept is similar: Each of us has certain strengths and weaknesses that have been adapted over time to maximize learning. Whether there are four or six different learning styles, eight or ten kinds of intelligence, the idea is that every student has particular talents and resources that favor verbal, spatial, logical, interpersonal, or other modalities. The more options we present, the more different modalities we access during teaching, the more likely it is that we can help students learn at their own pace, utilizing their own strengths, while fostering development in areas of weakness. Of course, this is one of those ideas that sounds good in theory but is incredibly difficult when juggling the individual needs, interests, personalities, and behavior of twenty, thirty, forty, or more children in a single classroom.

Relevance in Education

All children, from the most dedicated honors student to the most belligerent discipline problem, want to learn. The main challenge in education is not at all a matter of convincing our consumers that our product is worthwhile; rather, it is teaching subjects that they perceive as relevant and useful to them. Although we cannot always make all aspects of *schooling* relevant to students, we can make their *learning* more relevant to their lives.

What Students Want Most

Providing relevant learning experiences is one of the key features of effective classrooms. But don't take our word for it—listen to the voices of students. The following pleas for relevance in classroom learning experiences will not be too dissimilar from those of your own students.

Ask an elementary school child what he most wants to learn about in school, and he will tell you quite openly:

> *I don't like learning about periods and question marks and multiplication problems and stuff like that. I like learning about things that are more interesting. For example, when I'm playing computer games and I press the button to make a figure on the screen jump, how does that work? All the information goes from the remote controller to the console. But what happens after the information goes there?*
>
> *Drugs are something else I wouldn't mind knowing about. Where do they come from? How are they made? If they are supposed to be so bad for you, how come some people say they feel so good?*
>
> *I've got a whole long list of other things I wish we could learn about in school instead of the boring stuff we have to study. How can I dribble the basketball better with my other hand? How can I get my mom to let me stay up later at night? How can I have more friends sleep over? How can I get my older sister to stop bothering me? How can I make some money so my parents don't have to work so hard and could come home early? How do I prove myself to other people? I would love to know the answers to these questions.*

A middle school child is asked the same question: "What would you like to learn in school?" She responds instantly, as if she has been thinking about that very question her whole life:

I wish the teachers would just not talk so much and let us have more time to read. I wish we could go to any class we want. I want to learn about how to do magic tricks and play the piano better and have more friends. I wonder why people don't melt and why donuts have holes in them. I would like to learn how to work a compass and find my way back home if I got lost.

A high school student answers the question with equal fluency:

I would really like to understand what I can do to get girls to like me. I wish I could figure out what they really want. I want to know a whole lot more about love and sex. First of all, how do I get someone to have sex with me, and second, what is most important to girls about it? I would like to know how to have more friends and be more popular. I wish I could learn how to get my parents to stop fighting. I want to know what I'm going to do when I get out of this place—how I'm going to find a good job. I would love to learn more about fixing cars. I've got this transmission problem; the gears are always slipping.

As these three typical children have testified, there is indeed no shortage of things that almost anyone would like to learn about. The problem, however, is that we are mandated to teach subject areas that have not been selected by our consumers but rather by their guardians. So when we teach math and history and handwriting and grammar and economics, we must explain why they are included in the curriculum, why they are important, and connect them to students' daily lives. Furthermore, as mentioned above, teachers are under increasing pressure to improve performance on basic competency tests, which reduces their freedom even more.

Did anyone ever explain to you why you spent endless tedious hours learning to diagram sentences? To this day, can you tell the difference between a subject and predicate? Did any teacher ever sufficiently convince you of the value of proving geometric theorems, or balancing algebraic equations? Did you ever stand at the board, chalk or marker in hand, utterly befuddled—not only as to how to do what the teacher asked but, more important, why you should invest any energy in learning to do so? Did you ever wonder why you bothered to learn math, with all the memorizing of times tables and completing of pages of long division problems, especially since there were computers and calculators to serve those functions? It was not until much later that many of us realized that math is the basis of logic and problem solving and finally appreciated its relevance.

What can be seen from reading these examples of what children want to learn in school is that there is a gigantic discrepancy between their interests and what they actually spend their time studying.

Another problem has to do with the implicit but unintended messages that children pick up during their educational career. What is it that children really learn in school? They hear and interpret messages like the following:

- Learning is not what is most important; getting good grades is, pleasing the teacher is. Staying out of trouble is what counts.
- They should feel humiliated, frustrated, and stupid when they do not know the answer to a question. When they do not know or understand something, they should keep their mouths shut.
- They should not get caught cheating; but if they can get away with it, they will not only save themselves time and improve grades, but they will beat the teacher at his own game.
- They should blend in and not make waves or create disturbances.
- Only the teacher says things that are worth remembering; nobody ever takes notes on what another student says—it will not be on the exam.
- There are such things as right answers, even if they do not exist outside the classroom.
- It is winning that counts, definitely *not* how you play the game.
- You should not work to satisfy yourself but to please others.
- School is a prison, learning is boring, and education is a drag.

These negative attitudes can and must be addressed and counteracted if meaningful learning is to take place. The key is to make certain that what you are teaching and how you are teaching it is perceived by learners as being relevant to their lives and helpful to reaching their personal goals.

Teacher-Related Obstacles to Learning

For a teacher, it is important to understand not only how learning takes place but also what may impede or block it. Sometimes these obstacles create temporary barriers to student learning; sometimes the barriers are permanent.

Coercion, threats, and fear of negative consequences, all too common in our schools, are major barriers to student learning. We have seen all too often instances in which students are terrified to raise their hands, ask a question, or respond to a query because they don't feel it is worth the risk of humiliation or looking stupid. Before most students respond or speak up in class, they first rehearse exactly what they want to say and then try to anticipate any possible risk that might result. By the time they've worked up the courage, you've likely moved on to something else. It's no wonder that classrooms feel like such threatening places to many students.

It shouldn't be too difficult for you to draw on your own experiences as a student to confirm these statements. How well did you do in your classes during those times when it felt as if a threatening, critical authority figure was waiting to pounce on your every mistake? The problem is even worse when you feel, as we often do, that essentially you are a fraud and if you really reveal yourself, others will find out and reject you.

Shame is a cousin of coercion and also reduces the likelihood of learning. The "shame on you" taunts of parents, teachers, siblings, and peers often result in diminishing the self-esteem of students. Without self-confidence, many students experience chronic school failures. These disappointments, in turn, beget more shame.

Fear of shame frequently results in teacher-pleasing behaviors that have little to do with meaningful learning. High achievers seek to do perfect schoolwork to avoid being embarrassed by teachers or parents. They attempt to avoid failure at all costs because they feel their very survival is at stake. One of your main challenges as a teacher is both to provide your students with opportunities for success in their learning efforts and to assist them in coping with failure. In taking risks, in venturing into the unknown, in experimenting with new skills or ideas, it is inevitable that human performance will fall short of high expectations. Depending on how children deal with their mistakes, misjudgments, and imperfections, they will either become creative problem solvers and fearless truth seekers or, all too commonly, cautious academic achievers who become obsessed with grades and the approval of others. Unfortunately, this is one lesson in life that is all too often generalized to other areas.

In many classrooms for the so-called gifted and talented, another obstacle to learning may be found in the form of a competitive atmosphere. These budding scholars feel driven (or are driven by others) to succeed at all costs. They will accept no grade less than an A. Their teachers encourage them always to "strive to be the best."

Well-intentioned as the competitive learning climate and slogans of excellence may be, they are often translated in students' minds as, "Don't try anything unless you are certain you can do it well, and preferably better than anyone else." If learning is measured in terms of grade point averages and standardized test scores, these students may be considered academic superstars. Unfortunately, these same students are often rigidly conventional in their thinking, afraid of taking risks, interpersonally insensitive, and emotionally immature.

Contrast this learning environment with remedial classrooms composed of "low-ability" or "brain-dead" students, or "losers" as they are described by their peers. These children feel they have nothing to lose. They could not care less about the threat of F grades as motivators to learning. They have endured so much custodial teaching (the stay-in-your-seat, fill-in-the-blanks, and keep-quiet mode of teaching) that only one strategy can motivate them to learn: providing them with something significant and important to them as people.

> *In one such self-contained class of seventh-grade low-ability students, these often-belligerent students walked into their fourth period class as the teacher was putting away some new video camera equipment provided for his third period academically talented class.*
>
> *"How come we never get to make movies, Mr. Zehm, ain't we gifted students too?"*
>
> *"You know I think you've all got lots of smarts," Mr. Zehm responded with obvious embarrassment, "but I'm not allowed to use the equipment with this class. Now, let's work on our spelling lists today."*
>
> *The next day at the beginning of fourth period, the teacher was dumbfounded when the students proudly pranced into his classroom with two video cameras and a bag filled with cassettes. "You ain't got no excuse now, Mr. Z.," they confidently proclaimed. "We want to make our own movies now."*
>
> *During the course of the following month, these students, largely written off by the system, produced a high-quality video on a theme about which they were experts. "We want to make a movie about all the hassles we got . . . everybody hassles us!" That is exactly what they did. They were motivated to improve their reading so that they could follow the video camera instruction books. They wrote and revised their script over and over until it said exactly what they wanted it to say. These students made many mistakes, learned from them, and did what the experts in Hollywood did: They did as many retakes as they needed until they were satisfied with a particular scene or piece of dialogue.*
>
> *Mr. Zehm's so-called gifted students were not so successful. They were unable to take the risks needed to be successful. Their fear of failure compelled them to shadow him, seeking his approval. "Is this right, Mr. Zehm? Did I do this the right way?" He came to realize that many of his academically talented students were high achievers whose academic work was permeated with fear of failure, fear of getting any grade lower than A. These students needed help taking academic risks on their own.*

Beliefs Promoting Learning

In reading these case examples, you are likely considering your own ideas about what leads some children to do well in school and others to fail miserably. It is a good idea to monitor continuously your own beliefs about learning. Although many theories have already been produced, most of us have a sense that none of them really captures the essence of what takes place. The process is often so complex, so multidimensional, so uniquely constructed for each student in each situation, that it is virtually impossible to summarize what happened with any real confidence.

Think about a time in your life in which you experienced a major breakthrough in learning something significant that remains with you today. This could have been a new intellectual or conceptual insight that changed the way you think about the world, or some aspect of your discipline. It could have been a long-standing problem in your personal life that finally resolved itself as a result of something you learned. It could have been any transformative, seminal experience that forever changed you and the way you look at yourself. This could have occurred in a classroom, but more likely it happened during a situation in which you faced some adversity, dealt with some conflict, or otherwise struggled with a chronic issue that plagued you.

As you reflect on this significant learning process, what is your best understanding of what happened and why? How is it that after so many previous trials, so many hours, months, or years of frustration, you finally mastered this new skill or concept? How do you account for the learning taking place in that particular context or situation? What got through to you in a way that nothing had previously?

There are all kinds of possible explanations related to readiness, reinforcement, or a hundred other variables, but ultimately you have developed your own ideas about the best way to promote learning in others, especially when they are a bit reluctant or less than enthusiastically motivated. You have developed your own set of beliefs that guide your journey as a teacher. Perhaps they include some of the following:

- I believe that *all* of my students are curious, natural learners.
- I believe that *all* of my students are capable of learning.
- I believe that my students learn best when I actively involve them in relevant learning.
- I believe that my students learn best when I provide them with a safe and stimulating learning environment.
- I believe that my students learn best when I involve them in significant learning experiences that are as close to "real life" as I can get them.
- I believe that learning is personal, so I frequently get out of the way to encourage their authentic, personal responses.
- I believe that learning is social, so I provide lots of opportunity for students to work together in cooperative groups.
- I believe that language is central to thinking and learning, so I invite my students to actively participate in a classroom alive with opportunities to read, write, talk, listen, and share.

- I believe that modeling is a powerful tool for learning, so I continue to grow personally and professionally as an enthusiastic lifelong learner.

It's pretty clear that learning is a process that is not at all synonymous with many activities that take place in school. Although there are many different conceptions that explain how learning occurs, most of them agree on the importance of making the experience as dynamic and relevant as possible. This is far more likely to take place when we have developed a style of teaching that not only meets students where they are, connecting to their interests, but also reflects our unique personalities, strengths, and resources.

ACTIVITIES AND APPLICATIONS

1. Identify students who have a history of poor performance and achievement in school, perhaps those who are also dispirited and unmotivated. Interview them about what is most difficult for them and listen carefully and respectfully to their stories about how they became so marginalized. Note that even though they will tend to externalize the causes and blame others for their problems, they will also provide valuable information that will be useful to you when working with students in the future. Treat these students as experts on their own experience and valuable teachers for *you*. Even though they have all but given up, ask them what could possibly turn things around (This conversation might be part of that!).

2. Administer a learning-style inventory or multiple intelligences survey to a group of students after talking to them about what these differences mean and how they affect optimal learning. Share your own learning style(s)/preferences with them and talk about how such self-knowledge has helped you to adapt your own learning. Discuss the results of their inventories with respect to identifying strengths and weaknesses. Given such a broad range of styles, talk to peers about the challenges of addressing all these particular differences with such a large group of students under your care.

3. Discuss with colleagues how to encourage students to take "constructive" risks in the classroom, to disagree respectfully with a particular idea presented or to express opinions that may be different—or, for some students, just to raise their hand and say *anything* in a large group. Talk about how to deal with the inevitable disappointments, mistakes, failures, and shame that are associated with such risks.

4. Describe your personal beliefs about how you think learning best occurs. We are not talking about just *any* learning, but rather the kind of significant learning that continues to this day. Consider some of the most powerful and enduring learning experiences you've had in your own life. What is your best understanding about how this happened? Why do you suppose these particular experiences lasted so long while others did not?

4

Helping Relationships

> *Close your eyes for a moment. Take a breath—a deep breath. Consider the child sitting opposite you. Meet this child's eyes. Concentrate. Concentrate with all your being on this child. Use all your energy and power to focus completely on this person. Resist all other distractions, both internal and external. Attend to this child fully, using your body, gestures, eyes, smile. Use every part of your being to communicate that you care deeply about this child, about what is being said. Assure the child of your undivided attention, your acceptance, your caring.*

These instructions form the barest glimmer of what is involved in a helping relationship. It is so rare that any of us feels truly heard and understood by another person. In so many of our relationships, with family, friends, the people we are closest to, we sort of half-listen as we do other things simultaneously—check for texts or e-mails, answer the phone, glance at the paper, watch television, listen to the radio, stare out the window, wave to someone else passing by. We are all so hungry for someone to really listen to us—children most of all.

Ms. Chavez is a high school Spanish teacher. As one of the newer members of the staff, though by no means the youngest, she is assigned to teach the introductory language courses—sections that are required for high school graduation for sophomores at her school. Many of these students are not particularly interested in learning the language that Ms. Chavez has devoted her professional life to studying. Except for the minority who hope and plan to go to college, the rest of the students rarely do any homework or study for any exams.

Although the vast majority of the kids do not like studying Spanish, they do like and respect their teacher. They say she seems to be a nice enough lady and she seems to care about them. She stays after class to talk to them. She makes an effort to get to know each of them. She even tells them things about her own life and she is friendly when she talks to them.

When Wendy got pregnant, when Kyle was kicked out of the house, or when Mick came to school with a broken nose, Ms. Chavez was the first adult they could think of to talk to. She always listened to students without judging them or telling them what to do; instead she tried to be supportive and to help them to figure out things for themselves. Most important, they trusted her. When she suggested seeing their counselor or having their parents come in for a conference, they might not follow through, but at least they would listen.

Word eventually got out that Ms. Chavez was "alright." She might teach Spanish, and she might be a tough disciplinarian, but class would often be fun. Her students, when questioned as to what they liked most about her, would unhesitatingly mention that they felt close to her. At basketball games or school concerts, she was among the first people that students would seek out to greet.

Ms. Chavez acknowledges she has quite a following in the school, and she attributes it to a single factor—the time and effort she spends getting to know the kids who will let her get close to them. As Ms. Chavez clearly demonstrates, it is through our relationships with children that we earn their trust. Once they have decided that we are adults worthy of their respect, they will follow us wherever we might wish to lead them, from the Peloponnesian Wars, Pythagorean Theorem, and past participle to Picasso, Plato, and Pizarro. Most children could care less *what* we teach as long as they feel connected to us in some intimate and respectful way. Whereas this might seem rather obvious, the more years we spend in the profession the more likely we might forget that it is sometimes the simplest things we do that make the greatest difference to our students.

STUDENTS' PERCEPTIONS OF CARING RELATIONSHIPS

One of the most important facets of effective teaching relationships has to do with providing support and regard for students. Sure, students need structure and discipline, but they also respond to those who they know genuinely care about them. As mentioned in the case of Ms. Chavez, students are even willing to do work that they don't actually value if they feel that the teacher has made a connection with them. They are also inclined to feel a more positive attitude toward their school experience and its unique culture when there is some empathic connection to a teacher.

What do students consider important in the caring relationships their teachers establish with them? The results are often surprising in that it isn't just a matter of being "nice" or "easy to talk to." Students feel cared for when the class is managed effectively, when they can depend on the teacher to keep things safe, orderly, and inviting. This is often just as important as evidence of compassion and caring. Students are big on the perception of fairness, that everyone is treated the same, without obvious favorites. Even those who are sanctioned or punished don't mind as much if they believe that others are treated the same way, that they haven't been singled out for reasons that aren't apparent or deserved. And when students do cross a line or act inappropriately, they especially appreciate teachers who are forgiving and give them the benefit of the doubt.

Students also recognize teachers as caring when the teachers genuinely express concern for them. This is especially the case when teachers extend themselves in some way such as by offering encouragement and support during difficult times. They show an interest not only in the students' schoolwork, but in their personal lives. They remember things that are important to their students and follow up on previous conversations.

"So, Guillermo," a second-grade teacher says in greeting one of his students as he walks into school. "I see you're here early this morning. That must mean it was a tough night last night with all your cousins visiting. Bet you couldn't wait to get out of there as soon as you could?" The little boy nods shyly but smiles in appreciation for being recognized.

Ms. Wilkes is sitting at her desk as her fourth-hour sophomore English class files in just under the last bell. As one girl quickly slips by her desk, the teacher remarks to her, "Good game you had last night. I saw you scored a goal and got two assists." The teacher knows that it is a big deal to this student to be starting on the varsity soccer team, especially since it is about the only area of her life that is currently going well.

"Thank you, ma'am," she says, half with pride and half with embarrassment. She rolls her eyes as she looks toward her friends, but she is more than a little pleased that her teacher noticed how well she was doing, especially since she was struggling so hard in this English class.

In both of these two cases, simple remarks communicate to the students that the teachers care enough about them to remember what is most important to them. Of course, this is not enough, but it is a good foundation for everything else you do.

Finally, students also feel that a strong dimension of teacher caring is related to the quality of their teaching. They recognize a caring teacher as one who makes learning interesting and understandable, relevant and engaging. They also feel caring teachers refrain from embarrassing students publicly in front of the whole class.

HUMAN DIMENSIONS OF HELPING RELATIONSHIPS

Human beings were designed to function in tribes—small, intimate groups that worked and lived together in mutual cooperation. Each of us had dozens of caregivers because all adults parented and mentored all the children of the tribe. The education of the children was the responsibility of the elders, who taught us how to hunt and forage and to take care of ourselves and everyone else. Every member of our society developed strong interconnected bonds; we depended on one another to survive.

Now, the tribes have been disbanded. Our families and childhood friends are scattered across the continent. Most human contact takes place through social media, mobile devices, and text messages. People live miles from where they were born and where they have their ancestral roots. We barely know our neighbors, much less engage them in intimate, supportive relationships.

Children are now taught by strangers called *teachers* and taken care of by guardians called *babysitters*. Rather than having face-to-face contact, with all the accompanying visual cues and "felt sense" of physical prox- imity, we are now spending more and more time developing relationships through technological portals.

It is the warmth and nurturance of human relationships that we all long for and that children most easily respond to. Learning most easily takes place in the context of a safe environment in which people feel secure enough to experiment, to take risks, to venture beyond their capabilities into the great unknown. Teachers who consistently respond with genuine warmth will, in the long run, be able to establish trust with even the most belligerent students. The relationships that we develop with children are the foundation of this learning environment, alliances that have certain defin- able characteristics.

IMPROVING RELATIONSHIP SKILLS

Although trust is a central ingredient of helping relationships, it is not enough. Teachers who are effective helpers have developed a repertoire of qualities and skills that support their efforts to be helpful and influential. They evaluate their communication skills to improve their classroom interactions; they conduct frequent checks on reality to assess the quality of their helping relationships.

Let us assume that you agree that the teaching relationship is indeed the basis for learning in the classroom or in any other setting. How, then, do you develop the skills, qualities, knowledge, or whatever it takes to create these alliances? Developing effective teaching relationships initially depends primarily on two factors: (1) the attitudes that you communicate to others, and (2) your proficiency in communication skills.

Helpful Attitudes and Helping Behaviors

Think about your times of greatest need, when you were really having problems and needed help. You struggled with a thorny issue, one with some difficult challenges. In deciding whom you would approach for assistance, whether it would be a close friend or relative, a coach or teacher, or a counselor, you reviewed in your mind whom *you* could trust the most. This means not just someone you could trust to keep things confidential and private, but also someone who would not judge or criticize you or attempt to impose his beliefs on you. You preferred someone who could listen to you, who would really hear you and then help you to find your own way through the difficulty. This is exactly the sort of attitude that everyone else would want in a helper as well, whether in a counselor's office or a classroom.

Now, when someone is turning to you, before you ever open your mouth, there are myriad internal tasks that must be completed to create a helping relationship. These include things related to the state of mind you adopt, one that is distinctly different from that of other relationships. Once you have decided to be helpful to another, a whole set of rules begins to operate that is otherwise dormant.

First, you must clear your mind of all distractions and focus your concentration on the person(s) you are helping. Give the student your complete and undivided attention, communicating with your eyes, your facial expressions, your posture, and body position, every part of your being showing that you are intensely interested in what this person has to say. Beginning helpers often discover, much to their surprise, that this simple act of deliberate attending to another person is often enough to help the person to open up. It is so rare, after all, that we ever have anyone else's undivided attention.

Picture a typical classroom scene in which a student cautiously approaches a teacher at her desk. The teacher is obviously busy assessing assignments and posting grades on a computer. She is hurrying to complete the task so she can use her usual preparation period to catch up on some other work she has to do. Yet here stands this child waiting for some attention:

> *"Yes, Maggie," the teacher says with impatience, "what can I do for you?"*
>
> *"Well, um, I guess it's not that important. It can wait until another time." The teacher looks up from her papers, pausing her fingers on the keyboard.*
>
> *"No, that's okay, what do you want?" As the child starts to speak, the teacher's eyes flick down toward her unfinished work.*
>
> *"It's just that there's been some stuff going on and I'm not sure what to do about it."*
>
> *"Go on," the teacher prompts. She is saying all the right things, encouraging the student to speak what is on her mind, but her nonverbal behavior and attitudes are communicating something other than complete interest.*

Take time to notice in all the conversations you have during a typical day how often people (and you) are doing other things—looking around, waving to others, checking messages, answering calls, rearranging clothes—at the same time that they (or you) are talking. Similarly, notice how wonderful it feels to speak to someone who is doing everything in her power to communicate that she is hanging on your every word. She is using her eyes, her smile, her head nods, and verbal acknowledgments to show that she is indeed following you closely.

Attending to the Speaker

You are clear. You feel neutral and open. You have focused your concentration on the task at hand. You are attending fully to your learner(s). You take a deep breath and you begin. If only it were this simple! In fact, when professionals use relationship skills, there are no fewer than sixty different behaviors involved. Most of these can be divided into several broad categories, each of which follows logically from its predecessor. Although some of these may seem rather simple and obvious, you'd only have to look around you at most conversations to notice how rarely people truly give one another their full attention.

We present a summary of some basic things for you to keep in mind when building relationships with students (see Table 1).

Table 1.   A Checklist of Things to Remember When Talking to Students

Your attitudes
• Stay clear
• Be nonjudgmental
• Feel accepting
• Act authentically
• Practice compassion
Your nonverbal behaviors
• Pay attention
• Maintain eye contact
• Communicate interest with face and body
• Express warmth
Your strategies
• Demonstrate support
• Show empathy
• Prove you have heard and understood
• Keep your focus on the student

Acceptance of Students Without Judgment

For children to open up and trust you, they must feel that you accept them as people, that you are relatively nonjudgmental and noncritical of them as human beings. This does not at all mean that you accept everything that *they* might say or do; on the contrary, there may be many things *about their behavior* that you find unacceptable or inappropriate. The point is that you are able to separate your disapproval of what children are doing from who they are as persons.

This nonjudgmental attitude is even manifest in the way you speak to children. Instead of implying that you dislike them because of what they are doing, you may wish to word admonishments *very* carefully and sensitively: "Carlos, I don't like what you're doing right now, and I need you to stop." It is crucial for Carlos to feel that although you will not tolerate his acting out in class, you still genuinely care for him and accept him as a person.

This may very well be one of the most difficult aspects of helping in general—and of teaching in particular—for acceptance of others requires a great deal of tolerance, sensitivity, and cultural awareness. It means that you are knowledgeable about the diverse backgrounds from which your students originate and that you demonstrate respect for their individual and cultural differences. When you can model this in your own behavior, then you can teach children to be tolerant of one another's differences.

Postponing Your Own Agenda

The commitment to be helpful to a child means putting your own needs and issues aside. It means doing anything and everything in your power to help the child reach his or her goals (as long as they are constructive). It means separating what is good for you versus what is good for the child, because sometimes these needs do not coincide. A teenager, for example, may be struggling with the decision to have an abortion and may have decided to follow through on this choice, even though you strongly object to abortion on moral grounds. With a friend or family member, it is perfectly fine to express your opinions in the most passionate terms, but in a helping relationship, you work within the student's value system, not your own. What you would do with your life is not often relevant to what your students should do with theirs.

This quality of helping relationships is so difficult to develop that counselors and therapists undergo years of training and supervision. Even so, in your work as a teacher, you are called upon to play a limited role in helping your students with personal issues, mostly listening and supporting, occasionally making referrals to qualified experts. If you think you already have enough to do, you are right. In Asia and other cultures where there are no counselors in schools, teachers are called upon to serve those roles in addition to other responsibilities. Furthermore, you could easily make a case that if a child does have a problem, the teacher is actually the one best positioned to intervene and is likely to be the initial adult in whom the child seeks to confide.

Although it is neither your job nor part of your training to do counseling, you will have numerous opportunities to make a significant impact on students' lives through the helping relationships you create with them. Being a teacher involves so much more than imparting wisdom and information; it means being available and accessible to students when personal issues are interfering with their ability to concentrate and excel in school.

What sorts of issues may come your way while you sit at your desk grading papers? This is but a sampling:

- "Nobody ever wants to play with me. They always tease me and call me 'turtle brain.' Can I stay inside and help you today?"
- "There is this girl I like, sort of, but she won't talk to me."

- "Ms. Rainey won't ever call on me. She thinks I'm stupid."
- "Nothing I do is ever good enough for my dad."
- "My uncle touches me sometimes, like in the middle of the night."
- "I don't know why I keep forgetting my homework."
- "Nobody ever picks me to play on their team."
- "My parents always nag me to clean up my room. That's all they ever do, nag, nag, nag."
- "Some of my friends think that I might be drinking a little too much. They think I should talk to somebody about it."
- "My mommy and daddy scream so much that it sometimes hurts my stomach."
- "I don't want to go to college."
- "How do you know if you're gay or not?"

In every one of these situations, you will be called upon to offer support and be caring; to be a good listener; and, most of all, to build trust. For you to offer this sense of comfort and nurture, children must feel that they are safe when talking to you.

THE HELPING PROCESS

To encourage others to find you attractive and approachable, trustworthy and safe, there are several skills you can learn that are part of the overall helping process. You can make a tremendous difference in students' lives by spending only a few minutes each day listening and responding to them. To do so, you must first understand how helping relationships are different from other encounters.

Assessment

In the first stage of the helping process, you listen and look at the student so that you can accurately observe and hear what is being communicated. Your job is not to diagnose and fix problems that are presented to you; rather, it is to help the children do this for themselves. The first and foremost set of skills that help you to hear what is being said, to collect relevant information about the presenting concern or complaint, and to make sense of what a person really means is called *attending behaviors*. This process of active listening is not as easy as it sounds.

Before children even open their mouths, you first set in motion a series of internal adjustments inside your head that permit you to be receptive. Earlier we talked about the attitudes that help you to remain clear and neutral. This means clearing your mind of distractions—things you have done or will do later, a grumbling stomach, or things going on around you. To enter a helping process means making a commitment to giving a person your full concentration without interruption. Sometimes this simple action, in itself, is experienced as healing by people with problems, because they just want a sounding board against which to bounce their ideas or feelings. This internal climate inside your head involves reminding yourself to stay nonjudgmental, to focus concentration, and to take that deep cleansing breath that keeps you centered.

In this initial stage of helping, you are attending both mentally and physically. You are not sitting behind a desk; on the contrary, you are doing everything you can to remove all barriers, physical or psychological, between you and the child. You are using eye contact, facial expressions, and body postures to communicate that this child to whom you are speaking is the most important person in the world to you at that moment in time. The child revels in your attention and feels nurtured by your soothing energy.

We invite you to experiment with these attending behaviors in your current personal relationships. During the next few days, pay particular attention to how you relate to your friends. Practice giving them your undivided attention. Use your eyes, body posture, head nods, and smiles to let them know you are hanging on their every word. Note what a difference such simple changes make in the quality and intimacy of your interactions.

You still have not opened your mouth or begun the interaction process, yet you are running through a mental checklist just the way a pilot would do before takeoff. You check your attitudes to make sure you are clearheaded, respectful, authentic, and compassionate. You heighten your sensitivity to what is unfolding by actually entering a meditative, altered state of consciousness that allows you to see and hear things just beneath the surface of ordinary reality.

This very state is what permits therapists to appear to read minds. Expert helpers have taught themselves to concentrate so intently on what is taking place that they are able to pick up cues that are invisible to the less informed. A child says, "I don't have a problem," but you hear a subtle nuance that tells you something different. A child's imperceptibly blinking eyes, flushed face, and quivering lip give valuable clues as to what is going on inside, signs that can be read and interpreted, given practice.

Most of the skills we are discussing in this chapter cannot be learned by merely reading about them; you must find ways to practice them to the point where they become relatively natural. Some of you may decide to pursue additional training.

Exploration

When you have given students your full attention, they feel encouraged to tell you what is going on in their lives. Your job in this second stage of helping is to gently facilitate the process of self-awareness—that is, to help them become more aware of what is going on inside themselves, as well as what is going on around them. We use our helping skills to facilitate their exploration of the internal and external world.

What this looks like in a classroom situation involves a teacher paying attention not only to the *content* of what is being communicated but also to the underlying *process* of the message. In the following example of promoting exploration of feelings as well as thoughts, a teacher helps her class to explore their deeper reactions to a discussion on conflict related to characters in a story they were reading:

Teacher: So, what many of you seem to be saying is that you think it's wrong for someone to argue for his or her ideas if it means hurting someone else.

Megan: Not exactly. I mean, in the story we read, the person just had to say something. And she wasn't being listened to, so she had to do something to get their attention. She didn't mean to hurt anyone.

Teacher: What about you, Megan? What about a time in your life when someone's feelings got hurt as a result of something you said? You didn't mean to be hurtful. You just tried to get your point across.

Megan: Yeah. That happens a lot with my sister.

Teacher: What about some others of you who can think of times in which this has happened?

Michael: I remember one time when you hurt my feelings by cutting me off.

The class breaks out in laughter. Michael tucks his head under his arm in embarrassment:

Teacher: I agree with you, Michael. That's *a good* example of exactly what we're talking about. I was so much in a hurry to get through the lesson that I forgot to pay attention to how some of you were reacting to things I was saying and doing. So, in the story, how do they resolve their disagreement? And what can we learn from that to apply in our own lives?

In this scenario, the teacher is probing the students to make connections between events that took place in a story and those in their own lives. She is helping them to relate the themes to their lived experiences. And she is doing so using mostly exploratory relationship skills, asking a few open-ended questions and expanding the discussion to include process as well as content elements. This exploration quite naturally leads to some deeper levels of understanding.

Understanding

In the third stage of helping, some degree of *insight* or *understanding* is fostered. We challenge children to look critically, objectively, and sometimes emotionally at what they are learning. We present new ideas; we help them to articulate their concerns and confusion, and then facilitate the integration of these perceptions into their own thinking. This involves not only introducing them to concepts but also helping them to personalize the relevance of the material to their own lives in much the same way that we just illustrated. True understanding is not just something that we know intellectually; rather, it is something that we have made part of us, resulting in changes in the way we behave, reason, and feel about ourselves and others.

The transition from understanding to action cannot take place unless children are willing to get outside of their comfort zones. Teachers who are skilled at developing good relationships are able to encourage children to translate what they know into something they can do. Tanya, for example, is extremely shy. She is very well-behaved,—a teacher's dream, if that teacher likes obedient, passive children who sit quietly and rarely say anything. The theme in today's history class is "order and disorder in the universe." The kids have a lot to say about the subject; they understand only too well about the way chaos rules their lives—everyone but Tanya, that is, who usually sits serene and Buddha-like at her desk. But today she is writing furiously in her notebook. Something has hit home for her.

The teacher notices Tanya's uncharacteristic animation and invites her to share her perceptions aloud. She politely declines by averting her eyes and shaking her head. The lesson moves along. After class, Tanya slinks by the teacher's desk, but not before he asks to speak with her for a few minutes during his next prep period. In this one-on-one situation, she feels a lot more comfortable expressing herself and proceeds to do just that—unleashing a barrage of pent-up feelings about how helpless and frustrated she feels. Related to the theme in class, her home life is a model of disorder and chaos. She never knows what to expect when she gets home, who will be spending the night, or what kind of mood her family will be in.

The teacher gently prods Tanya to talk about the things she had written down during class, ideas that are quite perceptive. Her conclusion is that order can never be created from disorder without decisive action to disrupt the usual patterns. The teacher readily agrees and then asks her how that principle applies to her own life. At first she is puzzled, then her face lights up and then darkens again and she shrugs in frustration: How can she ever change things that are out of her control?

There are some things that are definitely within her control, however, most notably how she chooses to respond to the chaos around her, even in the very class that they are in. Tanya has developed a clear awareness of the problems, but that is not enough; she must find a way to incorporate this insight into her behavior so that she can function more effectively in her life. The place to start, the teacher gently suggests, is in class. "What would it take for you to overcome the chaos you feel inside and venture outside yourself far enough to reveal what you think and feel?"

As Tanya is helped to convert her understanding into action, so must all learning become incorporated in behavior. Teachers who have highly developed relationship skills are able to facilitate this process through the trust that they are able to create, a safety that invites children to experiment and to take constructive risks. In Tanya's case, it was her teacher's willingness to offer support that gave her the strength she needed to find her voice and break out of her shell.

There are many instances in which after a few conversations together, the teacher can help to promote some degree of insight by applying other skills. *Interpretation* is the attempt to uncover the underlying meaning of a pattern of behavior. *Confrontation,* when used carefully and diplomatically, can also be extremely useful in pointing out discrepancies between what people say they want versus what they do. Both of these interventions (along with others you have already learned) are evident in the following dialogue with Raúl:

Teacher: What can I help you with? [Open-ended question] You look upset about something. [Reflection of feeling]

Raúl: Oh, it's probably nothing.

Teacher: You are saying it's not that important, but it seems you are concerned about something that you want to talk about. [Reflection of content]

Raúl: I don't know why I act like such a smart-ass in your class. I just can't help it.

Teacher: One reason may be related to something you mentioned earlier when you said your parents acted so much nicer to each other when they were angry with you. [Interpretation]

Raúl: Well, that's sorta true, I guess.

Teacher: You sound hesitant about that now, and a little scared about what that might mean if it were true. [Reflection of feeling]

Raúl: Nah. I just don't think it's that big a deal.

Teacher: Let me know if this doesn't fit, but I'm a little confused. Just a few minutes ago, you were saying this was a very big deal, maybe the biggest deal in your life at this time. But now you're saying it doesn't matter. [Confrontation] It sounds like you are having some doubts about looking at this too deeply. [Reflection of content and feeling]

In this two-minute conversation, quite a lot was learned and explored. Given Raúl's ambivalence and hesitance about getting too far into this, it might very well be best to end the talk at this point and resume it at another time. It is often the case that you will not have very much time in your helping interactions with kids, a few minutes here and there. That is fine, since it does not take very long to communicate your continuing interest and concern for those who are having a hard time.

Action

Helping students to understand how and why they have difficulties can be useful but often is not enough. There are some people walking around who are severely dysfunctional, who understand why they are so messed up, but who still refuse to change in any fundamental way. Helping students to translate their insights into some form of action is thus crucial to constructive change.

In its simplest form, this stage can be initiated by asking the student, "So, what do you intend to do about your situation?" This places responsibility squarely on the child's shoulders and implies that (1) something can be done, and (2) it is up to the child to do it. The objective of this phase is to help the student to set realistic goals, create a plan to reach them, and then secure a commitment to follow through with what is intended.

Kim feels stymied in her efforts to make more friends, but she is determined to keep trying. She reaches out to her teacher for support. In a previous talk, she had the opportunity to express her anger and frustration and feelings of loneliness. She then felt safe enough to explore with her teacher what she might be doing to turn people off:

Teacher: Last time you talked about how difficult it is to make new friends since you moved to this school. How do you feel now?

Kim: I understand that sometimes I do come on too strong. And you're right the way you pointed out how I tend to reject kids before they can reject me. I would like to try doing things differently. Maybe I could be a little more agreeable the next time someone approaches me instead of scaring them away.

The skill of effective goal setting is the method by which you can help children to create objectives that meet the following three criteria:

1. They should be specific and describe in detail exactly what will be done, when it will be done, and how often it will be repeated.

2. They should be realistic and attainable objectives that can be reasonably completed within time limits. Make sure that kids do not bite off more than they can chew.

3. They should be mutually negotiated rather than prescribed by you. The last thing a student wants from a teacher is another homework assignment. It is far better to encourage the student to declare what she would like to do. That way, if the goal is not completed, it is the student's choice rather than a reaction to your intervention.

In the following conversation, a teacher is helping a second-grade child to work on some constructive action to overcome his chronic shyness:

Teacher: You were saying that it's not that you're shy in all situations, but just in school.

Student: Well, sometimes.

Teacher: You mean that there are times here in school when you aren't shy as well. For instance, you were telling me that when you are playing soccer during recess you're one of the first kids picked to play on a team.

Student: [Smiles] Yeah.

Teacher: You've also said that you'd like to do something about this problem. So, what do you want to do?

Student: [Shrugs]

Teacher: You're not sure what to do.

Student: I guess I could start talking more. Like in class and stuff.

Teacher: That's a great idea, but how could you go about doing that, since it's been so hard for you?

Student: Well, like in your class, I could talk more.

Teacher: Okay. Let's start small, with some little steps in the direction you'd like to go.

In this conversation, you will recognize the teacher using all of the preceding skills you have learned. First, the issue is clarified and the child's thoughts and feelings on the matter are labeled and reflected back to him. Resisting the urge to tell the student what to do (and often we think we know what will work best), the teacher instead slowly leads the child to declare his own "homework assignment" that will help him to act less shyly.

In the action stage of helping, your objective is to encourage students to plan ways in which they would like to be different. Your job is to talk them through the process of generating alternatives, narrowing the choices to a preferred course of action, and following through with the plan. Often, role playing and other rehearsal strategies can be especially useful in building confidence and giving the child practice experimenting with new behaviors in a safe environment. For example, a teacher might suggest, "You say that you are tired of waiting for boys to ask you out and that you would like to be the one to initiate relationships. Pretend that I am a boy you like. How would you approach me?"

In addition to skills you have in helping children think through problems, find solutions, and carry them out, through your support and encouragement you bring the helping process full circle back to the trust you established in the beginning. For although being a helper means that you are highly skilled in relationship building, communication, and problem solving, the essence of the process involves being perceived as trustworthy and safe to confide in. Supporting students to take action, from your perspective, particularly as a new teacher, may be for the students to get help from a professional.

Referrals to a Trained Professional

It is beyond the scope of your job, as well as your training, to plan and implement a series of interventions similar to those described above. Besides, you do not have the time or the energy to schedule regular sessions with kids on an ongoing basis; that, after all, is what professional counselors and therapists are for. But there is so much you *can* do to help children experience good, helping relationships, to offer support and encouragement, and to get them started on a path toward greater success and satisfaction. In such instances, your referrals are more likely to "stick," meaning that kids will be more inclined to follow your suggestions and seek the help they need. You have shown them not only that adults can be trusted, but also that adults can treat children with respect.

It's likely you will be faced with serious problems for which your skills are underdeveloped, areas in which you feel uncomfortable talking, such as lifestyle choices or pregnancy, or just too many demands on your time. In the best interest of the student(s), you need to refer them to someone else. School psychologists, school counselors, school social workers, and administrators are trained specialists.

Making a referral is not easy, especially when you have worked so hard to develop a relationship and want the relationship to continue. We suggest you let the student know that while you are pleased that the individual has come to talk to you about the concern and that you care about the student, you are not the best person to offer the help or guidance that is needed in this particular situation. As a result, you are referring him or her to a professional. It's important to carefully watch for the student's response so as not to "put off" the student. You offer support by providing contact information and explaining the counseling process (perhaps even pointing out how that process has already begun with the initial conversations you have had with the student). You can also follow up from time to time to see how things are going, again showing you continue to care about the student.

When a distraught teenage student confided in me (Ellen) that she was drinking a lot because she felt pressure from her family to join in with them as they sat around the television every weekend and drank beer, I was pleased that she trusted me enough to confide in me. I was also quick to learn that my helping expertise was limited and that I needed to find those sources of assistance in the community where my students and their families could receive confidential support. As a result of the relationship I had fostered with this girl, I was able to convince her to speak to her school counselor for additional help.

RELATIONSHIPS IN A TEACHER'S LIFE

The true beauty of these relationship skills is that they are applied with equal effectiveness to all human connections, including those with your colleagues, friends, and family members. Once you make yourself into a relationship specialist, supremely skilled at developing trust and safety with those whom you help, there is no reason you cannot do so as well in other areas of your life.

It never ceases to amaze us how hypocritical some members of our profession can be. As teachers, we supposedly are models of wisdom and learning. Apart from any content we pass along, the human dimension of our job is to impart values of truth seeking, honesty, integrity, and compassion. Yet so often we see teachers who appear so "together" in their classes and so spectacularly ineffective in their lives. Or they cannot practice in their own lives what they say is so important for their students to do or to be. They preach in their classes about how valuable it is to study hard, but they no longer work with the degree of commitment that they expect from others. They demand that their students stretch themselves, yet they are doing essentially the same things they have been doing for a long time. They ask their students to be good citizens, to be kind and respectful toward one another, yet they are somewhat less than caring in the ways that they relate to others in their school. Not only do these discrepancies compromise their professional effectiveness, since students are incredibly aware of hypocrisy, but teachers also surrender such a wonderful benefit of the job: the opportunity, to apply relationship skills where they matter the most—with those you love.

If you have trained yourself to become an attentive and compassionate listener, just imagine how easily those habits can be translated into the natural ways you relate to everyone in your life. If you develop the ability to read students' nonverbal cues and innermost feelings, this interpersonal sensitivity becomes just as useful with loved ones. When you learn to present yourself in class as confident, knowledgeable, and influential, there is no reason why you cannot become more persuasive at home and with friends. The more skill and sensitivity with which you do your work at school, the more able you are to become a better friend, parent, partner, and colleague.

ACTIVITIES AND APPLICATIONS

1. Begin keeping a systematic record of the best practices related to creating and maintaining a positive classroom environment. Almost every practicing teacher has some favorites, and most are proud to share them. Find out which rules and norms they consider most critical and how they enforce them. Ask them about their preferred routines and strategies, how they deal with disruptive behavior, how they energize a classroom that is complacent, what they do when they feel stuck. Make it a personal priority and policy to collect the best suggestions to guide the development of your own practices in the future.

2. Honestly and critically consider your own ability and skills in building relationships with students. What are some of your strengths in showing them how you care about them and support their efforts? What are some areas of weakness that you intend to develop in order to make yourself more accessible and responsive to their needs?

3. With a partner, practice the attending and listening skills mentioned in this chapter. Take turns talking about an issue while giving the speaker your undivided attention. Watch the speaker's nonverbal behavior as well as listen to the words being said. Reflect back what you have heard to show you were truly listening and understand what was expressed.

4. Talk to a school counselor or a social worker about the types of problems commonly referred to their office. Review the referral process and consider what you will say to best support students. Practice role playing how to make a referral for a student in need.

5

Mentoring and Being Mentored

After seven years as a social studies teacher, I was feeling very comfortable in the classroom. I could easily develop lesson plans and teach. I enjoyed students and had my own set of effective classroom management strategies to go along with my teaching style. Then I moved to a new state, got a job at a new school, and I felt lost. I needed someone to inform me of the ethnic demographics of this school population and share the school's history. I needed an explanation of the school's traditions and cultures. I needed to know how to obtain supplies and resources, plan field trips, and engage local guest speakers. And I needed instruction on using the school's computer and software systems. Wow! I had a lot of questions! Fortunately, different people came to the rescue: a veteran who had been in the building for twenty years who knew the school culture, the department chair who had great materials and community contacts, and an experienced teacher who possessed current technology skills.

ASKING FOR HELP

There is a myth that some day we will know enough, and have enough skills, that we really understand what is going on most of the time and can deal with any situation that might arise. Although it is certainly true that experience makes the job much easier, one of the exciting (and frustrating) aspects of our profession is that it is far too challenging and complex to ever truly get a handle on everything going on. The dynamics of each classroom are often completely different: What worked in one situation or setting will fail miserably in another.

The varied personalities, interests, economics, resources, leadership, and a hundred other factors always present new situations for us to confront—many variations of what we've encountered before but others completely novel and foreign.

I (Jeffrey) have taught a freshman writing seminar for years, designed to help first-generation college students better succeed in their new environment. I've accumulated hundreds of fool-proof teaching strategies, engaging interactive exercises, cooperative learning activities, riveting lectures, multimedia, classroom structures, and time-tested responses to almost any situation that could possibly arise. Yet even with all that experience and confidence, I often feel clueless a lot of the time about what was really going on in the room. I have trouble reading student expressions. (Are they bored? Tired? Or just hiding their excitement?) They won't talk in class or even in small groups. They aren't doing their reading assignments. Several students are skipping class. I'm doing the same things I usually do but very little seems to be working. What's going on?

It is both humbling and disconcerting to realize that no matter how many years we teach, there is still so much more for us to learn. Just when we think we've got things under control, we face new challenges we've never imagined. And that's one reason why mentoring never ends. No matter how old you are, or how many years you've spent in the field, you will always need help from others who have expertise or knowledge in new areas; sometimes you just need a trusted confidante and listener who can hear you out.

We just can't possibly learn everything on our own, nor keep up with all the developments in pedagogy, technology, and popular culture, much less our students' lives. There is not a task more important than finding wise and experienced colleagues who can guide us throughout our careers and no role more important than the one we provide as mentors for others who are struggling. Each of us, no matter where we are positioned in our profession, no matter how old we are or how long we've been working in the field, needs support during times of confusion or crisis. And say what you will about a teacher's journey—we certainly get more than our fair share of challenges on a daily basis.

At times we are all protégés who admire selected others for their skills or ways of sorting through problems. Each of us seeks out individuals who hold a degree of wisdom or experience that augments our own knowledge; each of us serves that role for others. Teachers often seek mentoring help when they require specialized assistance. They will

- Gain the benefit of expertise that is outside their specialty
- Help them look at fresh or innovative solutions to problems that they face

- Get a more detached and objective perspective on what they are experiencing
- Solicit help handling tasks that they don't have the time or inclination to complete
- Obtain training or information in a particular area of need
- Find alternative perspectives that are creative or different
- Challenge patterns or behaviors that are counterproductive or ineffective
- Lend support during difficult times that have been sparked by personal issues or professional problems
- Act as an advocate on their behalf when under pressure or in transition

As highlighted in the example that began this chapter, we often need short-term support until we figure things out and function on our own, but we also benefit from long-term support. It was the department chair described above who became my (Ellen's) ongoing mentor. She not only facilitated my adjustment in a new position but also guided me professionally in succeeding years. She helped me in many ways, both big and small. For example, at the beginning, she would make a point to sit next to me at meetings and whisper background information on events in my ear. She would tell me the names and positions of the people who spoke up the most, explain who had the most power, and indicate who had negative attitudes. She had taught several of my students in the past, so we often talked about students who were difficult in class or at risk of failing, and what teaching strategies worked best with our school population.

Professionally, my mentor encouraged me to meet other people throughout the district and to join the state social studies council, two activities I had never pursued before. As a result, I volunteered to participate on the district textbook adoption committee. Then, when she invited me, I agreed to copresent a program at the state social studies conference on a teaching strategy we had successfully implemented with ninth-graders at the school.

When my mentor retired as department chair, she recommended me for the position. Once again, I found myself needing lots of assistance for this new role. Planning a schedule and submitting a budget, completing purchasing orders, and advocating for department supplies were brand-new tasks for me. She helped me navigate the personalities in my department when it came time to determine the next year's schedule. Fortunately, my mentor continued to provide assistance, expertise, and support after she left the school.

Our relationship continued over many years, and I still consider her one of the most important influences on my career. As I look back on all the ways she supported me, I realize that my own commitment to mentor new teachers stemmed so much from my own experiences as an educator who was so grateful for the guidance I received. In fact, those experiences led to a later career change to the district as a curriculum specialist.

THE VALUE OF SUPPORT

Many schools will pair a new teacher with a more experienced colleague, which is a good start (if the match is compatible). As well, people find their own mentors or begin mentoring informally. The mentor's job generally starts with guiding the newcomer through the maze of school routines, procedures, rituals, and required paperwork. My (Ellen) mentor also acquainted me with a variety of school norms and the reasons why they developed as they did. She immediately let me know about two unwritten ones: (1) that conversations at lunch about school were frowned upon as the faculty had worked very hard to have a nonduty lunch; and (2) most faculty left the building by 5:00 p.m., the time that custodians locked the building entrances. On a social note, she also welcomed me to join others for dinner at a local restaurant before attending football games as a group.

Even for those who have been working for years in a particular school, there are still times when a mentor can be absolutely critical to help us support students who present academic and behavior challenges; negotiate difficult transitions, such as moving to a new school; or face new challenges, such as teaching at a new grade level or class. Good mentors provide emotional support for and understanding of our experiences. We seek out someone we trust and respect, as well as one who can support our development; usually such relationships are mutually beneficial.

BUILDING THE RELATIONSHIP

Nathaniel was on the verge of quitting his job or else being fired—it wasn't clear which outcome was most likely. But what was clear was that this new teacher was totally discouraged and overwhelmed. He was one of the few men teaching in the school and felt totally marginalized not only because of his gender but also his ethnicity and socioeconomic background. He was bitter and defensive, and he mistrusted the senior teacher who had been assigned to him as his mentor.

What Nathaniel needed most was not advice or suggestions but support. He felt there was nobody he could talk to, nobody who really understood him, nobody who really cared about whether he succeeded or not; in fact, it felt to him as if the school was not a very safe place. As such, he was on the verge of switching careers. When he was asked by his assigned mentor what he wanted most, Nathaniel just shrugged. "I just want you. I want someone, anyone, to understand why this is so hard for me."

In this case, it turned out that the best course of action was for this new teacher to pursue options elsewhere, but when he left the school he did so on his own terms, feeling greater appreciation for what he learned about himself and his role as a teacher. He credits his relationship with this mentor and the trust that they developed in a relatively short period of time that provided him with the confidence and support to take constructive action instead of continuing to wallow in self-pity and helplessness. This collaboration was effective largely because of the quality of the relationship they developed, in which it felt safe to talk about difficult things without fear of judgment or criticism.

Whether in the role of protégé or mentor, it is important to set and abide by some guidelines so that each of you will know what to expect from each other and avoid disappointment. You can start by establishing a schedule for when and how long you will meet. It's also helpful to try to find a time and place where you will not be subject to interruptions.

Along with setting dedicated time, other guidelines to establish include:

- *Identify ahead of time the items you wish to discuss.* Without such thoughtful planning, the time may end up becoming socially enjoyable but not necessarily professionally helpful.
- *Agree on confidentiality.* A mentoring relationship has to feel safe for both parties; otherwise, it is difficult to talk about the things that matter most.
- *Respect each other's differences.* It is often interesting and stimulating to listen to points of view that are different from your own. But this only works if both parties are respectful of these conflicting opinions.
- *Stay focused on an agenda that is most useful.* Without such an explicit agreement, meetings can easily turn into gripe sessions that may feel good for a while, but ultimately may not prove very helpful.
- *Negotiate a mutually satisfying relationship in which support flows in both directions.* Recognize and allow that each person has contributions to make to and receive from the other as a result of the experience.

FACILITATING PROFESSIONAL GROWTH

Developing a meaningful and constructive relationship takes time and effort on the part of both the mentor and the person being mentored. Once that is in place, both parties can then work together to deepen their understandings of and improve their teaching practice in a process that results in professional growth for each. In the next section, we look at the responsibilities of and benefits for the participants, the importance of listening, and how to give and receive suggestions and feedback.

Protégé Responsibilities

Given that mentors are usually not paid much (if at all) for their role, it is important that their protégés live up to their own responsibilities in the relationship. These include acknowledging the help you receive and the progress you make. Most of all, follow through on what you say you will do, honoring the mentor's time by demonstrating that it has been worthwhile. And remember to show your appreciation!

A mentor relationship is reciprocal: It represents an exchange of ideas and support. Mentors will draw out from you what ideas and skills you can offer them and other colleagues as well. There may be areas related to technology or some teaching strategies that they may express an interest in learning. Or they may consult you on how best to develop relationships with today's students. Your background in working with diverse students may be the asset they were looking for. Frankly, our students are the best mentors we have with respect to social media and technological developments. In the last year alone, students tutored us in video editing, tweets and settings in social media, and even new bells and whistles that accompany updates to presentation software.

Benefits of Mentoring

It's exciting to work with new professionals who are eager to succeed, whether they are beginning or veteran teachers. We welcome them and help them become comfortable in our "home away from home." This is a new stage in our professional growth as we extend our influence beyond our own classrooms and guide them to find their place in the grade level or department.

One teacher shared, "I love working with first-year teachers. They are thrilled to have their own classroom and are just bursting with energy—it's contagious. Responding to their *What if's?* and brainstorming how to implement their ideas keeps me on my toes."

Being able to serve as a resource to others is not only a recognition of our achievement but also how we contribute to the school, district, and the profession. Our protégés may take on future leadership roles and even take over when we leave, as shown above. We are building for the future.

Mentors choose their roles not just because of some altruistic motive or responsibility they feel to help beginners and their students, but also because they realize they'll enjoy benefits from the relationship as well. One of the best ways to improve our own professional effectiveness is through the mind of a beginner who sees things through fresh eyes, who brings a level of exuberance to the job, not to mention updated knowledge that may challenge our own most cherished assumptions. Beginners reteach more experienced professionals about the power of hope and enthusiasm before they become tempered with disappointments. They stimulate our increased passion for teaching, especially after years in the field when we might be inclined to take some things for granted.

It's All About Trust

Sure, experience, wisdom, and expertise are crucial qualifications for an effective mentor, but they won't mean very much if there isn't mutual trust in the relationship. It's difficult to ask someone a question, or solicit help, if you fear that you will be judged critically or that your disclosures won't remain private. It's difficult to open up to someone, especially about areas you feel most uncomfortable, if you don't feel a degree of acceptance and support.

Building trust is thus the first step in developing a collegial relationship. It doesn't happen all at once, or even very quickly, but it should be an explicit part of ongoing discussions. It is hard enough to admit to a senior colleague that you don't know what you're doing, that you feel confused or lost, but it is almost impossible when you sense that person might say or think the worst of you. It certainly helps when conversations include disclosures by both parties. In one sense, as authors we are operating as mentors for readers, which is why we choose to share our own stories with you that don't necessarily reflect heroic or brilliant actions as much as human ones. We have been frank and open in disclosing that even after so many years in the classroom we still don't always know what to do. We see it as a strength that we are willing to own and admit our ignorance and faults because it allows us to seek out others who can help us. Our hope is that this mutual sharing makes it easier for you to examine your own lapses and areas in need of improvement.

Perhaps the single most important way to build a trusting relationship is for the mentor to do a lot of listening, communicating clear understanding without the need to frequently interrupt, give advice, or overstructure the interaction. Teachers will frequently start the conversation with a specific question: "How do I find more chairs for my classroom?" "What happens after I submit a discipline referral form?" Whereas it is easy enough to respond with simple, specific answers—"In the storeroom . . . The dean will contact you . . ."—there are often deeper issues involved. In this case, the questions, fired one after the other, signal evidence of a lot of confusion and the teacher feeling overwhelmed. It is a good idea to address the presenting issues but also important to talk about what lies underneath them.

Knowing how tech-savvy current teachers are and how used they are to on-demand learning, I (Ellen) find e-mail a convenient way to respond to new teachers' needs, especially at the beginning of the year. I make a point to regularly look for their e-mails in my inbox. One of my protégés would write her lesson plans every Saturday morning and send them to me to review the objectives. I just made sure I checked that afternoon or sometime early on Sunday to see if she had sent a message. She was very appreciative of the opportunity to revise them before she taught. After a month, she was doing fine on her own and no longer needed weekly support for writing lesson plans. Technology helped take care of a number of practical concerns, but I still found it important to meet with her in person on a regular basis so we could talk about other issues that didn't lend themselves to simple, specific answers. Discussing classroom management, for example, merited face-to-face conversations.

New teachers are especially vulnerable to feelings of self-doubt (so are veteran teachers). Common statements you might hear are: "I just don't think I am connecting with Students X and Y. They barely make eye contact"; or "The last quizzes were not very good." Providing emotional support, encouragement, and reassurance help them to talk about their concerns, as well as open up new avenues that can be explored. This is especially important when working with minority teachers, who may be even more reluctant to talk about areas where they feel less than prepared or competent.

Giving Suggestions and Feedback

One of the most important tasks for a mentor is to provide honest, constructive feedback to new teachers on ways they can improve. The problem is that most people don't know how to provide such input in the most advantageous way so that it can be heard without defensiveness or withdrawal. Feedback is usually too benign ("You're doing a good job") or blunt ("That wasn't the smartest thing to do") to be helpful. And it is another one of those life skills that were rarely taught to us in a systematic way.

Usually feedback is conceptualized as either *positive* or *negative*. We find those labels to be counterproductive, especially considering that it isn't exactly clear what determines this classification. Is it really positive feedback to hear that you are doing a great job but offered no concrete, specific suggestions for how to improve? Is it really negative feedback if someone offers you potentially life-changing input about how you get in your own way, even though it's difficult to hear it?

Perhaps better labels for feedback are *supportive* and *constructive*. It turns out that the most effective feedback you can offer to someone is the kind in which they are given something concrete to work on and yet also feel that it was offered from a position of caring rather than criticism. In other words, the best feedback has certain elements:

- *It is presented in a caring, compassionate, and respectful way, with a supportive tone.* "I really appreciate how open you are to learning alternative ways to deal with this situation. Not everyone would have the courage and flexibility to look at this so honestly. And I really appreciate your trusting me enough to offer what help I can."

- *The constructive input should contain both areas of strength as well as things to improve.* "I know it really bothers you that you lost control, but it's also impressive that you recognized that about yourself. It seems as if that is an important first step to not letting this get underneath your skin when it inevitably happens again."

- *Feedback should be as concrete and specific as possible, with supporting examples.* "You mentioned that you don't like being in social situations, and it's true that sometimes you appear awkward. I noticed in the lounge that you often sit by yourself and don't make eye contact with anyone else. But I've also observed times when you do reach out to others. For instance, you quite assertively sought me out today to help you with this problem. If you can do that with me, I bet you can do that in other situations."

- *Rather than just giving advice (which is often not acted on, anyway) make sure the person has the opportunity to personalize and adapt the idea to his own style.* "I'm wondering how what I just told you fits with your experience? What part of what I shared with you strikes you as useful enough to do something with it?"

- *Avoid situations in which the other person feels the need to defend or explain herself.* "I notice that you are wanting to tell me why you acted that way, but the issue is really related to what it is about this that you'd like to change."

- *Collaborate and negotiate alternative solutions.* "I wonder what you could do instead to make a very different impression on those present, and yet also feel like you are protecting yourself?"

Whether you are giving feedback in the position of a teacher to a student, a mentor to someone you are helping, or in the context of any relationship, the first step is always to make sure that the other person is actually open to what you are offering. And it's difficult to ask directly ("Would you like some feedback?") because people will often lie and say, "Sure." But they really don't mean it, and they're not really listening.

In the end, as time progresses—and change can often be very slow—you will have the enviable position of recognizing and sharing in their successes: their students' accomplishments.

Accepting Suggestions and Feedback

One of the most challenging tasks for any of us, whether in a personal or professional situation, is to solicit and remain open to feedback from friends and colleagues. Let's face it: No matter how much we might hunger for honest input regarding our actions and behavior, it is really frightening, and even threatening, to face things about ourselves that are less than desirable. People say to others all the time things like, "Tell me what you really think," or "Do you have some suggestions for me?" but the truth of the matter is that we really prefer others just to tell us what we want to hear.

If trust has been established in the relationship, it's a lot easier to hear feedback without feeling defensive, criticized, or threatened. There are few gifts more valuable than having someone you trust tell you things about yourself that you may not know or understand.

Once trust and respect are established in the relationship, there is one opportunity even more helpful than hearing feedback after the fact—inviting the colleague to observe you in action. As nice as it might be to hear input based on your self-report, it is even more powerful and potentially useful to get feedback based on direct observation. It is quite different having a trusted colleague or friend watch you rather than an administrator whose job is to evaluate your performance.

Although I (Jeffrey) have been teaching for many years in many different settings and contexts, recently I was really struggling with a group of students who did not appear to be engaged and were not completing their work. Whereas initially I kept complaining about and criticizing their behavior, blaming them for the mediocre results, I finally had to accept some responsibility for the situation. As much as I wanted to figure out what I was doing that wasn't working, and what I could try differently, I kept hitting a brick wall. This had never happened to me before in quite this way, so it made it even easier to blame the students for their inertia and indifference. The more withdrawn they seemed, the harder I'd work at trying to engage them—with no visible results.

I invited two trusted colleagues to observe the class, and I specifically asked, even begged, for feedback on my behavior, not necessarily commenting on the students. It was after that observation that one of my colleagues drolly commented that I was working too hard, accepting too much responsibility for the outcome, and therefore not allowing the students to rise to the occasion. I heard other comments that were much more difficult for me to hear and accept—that I came across as pouty and punitive, that I was asking the students to do things for which they were unprepared, that I seemed inaccessible. At first, I was resistant to this feedback—that is, until my colleagues provided me with very specific examples of my behavior. It also helped that I really did trust that they had my best interests at heart.

Increasing Personal Effectiveness

In the context of evolving relationships, colleagues learn that the best teachers are lifelong learners throughout their professional journeys. The mentor models a spirit and attitude that even with years or decades of experience show there are always new challenges, always mistakes and failures to process, always opportunities to improve one's functioning—in the classroom, within the school culture, and in one's personal life. In fact, one of the gifts of becoming a teacher in the first place is that so much of what we learn to be more effective in our work also helps us to be more fully functioning human beings in our personal lives.

A new middle school math teacher told us how she went to her mentor, who happened to be the department chair, to ask for a pacing guide to help her with her long-range planning. In order for her students to do well on the benchmarks, she needed to know what algebra concepts would be covered on each test and when they would be administered. The mentor responded that neither the department nor the district had one but that she would contact the district curriculum specialist and offer to work on a committee to develop one as soon as possible.

A veteran high school math teacher explained how working with a new coteacher helped her do a better job in the classroom. The first-year teacher shared with her his ideas and some of the strategies he recently learned at the university in his teacher education program. She was able to observe him teach and thus expanded her instructional repertoire. Together they discussed the improvement in student achievement.

Ideal mentors model in their own lives that which they wish for their colleagues and their students. Credibility comes not just from knowledge and expertise but also by living these principles on a daily basis. We continue to learn and grow. We all aspire to become more calm, caring, compassionate, and knowledgeable—the extent to which we actually live these values in our everyday interactions is what gives us the power to influence others in positive ways. More than what we say to others, it is what we do that matters most.

ACTIVITIES AND APPLICATIONS

1. What is your current plan to identify, select, and recruit mentors to support your continued development? Unless you are prepared to take determined action, you may not benefit from the advantages of working closely with a senior colleague who is utterly trustworthy and has your best interests at heart. Once you negotiate such a relationship, what are some specific areas in which you would most like help?

2. Compare the best and worst mentoring experiences you have had in your life, whether they took place with a coach, teacher, supervisor,

relative, or someone else. What are the differences that stand out the most?

3. One of the most important roles of a mentor is to provide valuable feedback in a way that is easily received and digested. This means that it is offered in a way that is sensitive and caring yet also direct and honest, hopefully with specific examples. Practice giving and receiving feedback with a partner, starting with some rather simple and basic things.

4. Assess how being a mentor and/or being mentored has increased your personal, professional, and pedagogical effectiveness.

6

Working Within Student Cultures

Who are you?

However you would answer that question—as a teacher, a wife, a Christian, an Italian American, a woman, an athlete, a father, or any dozen other role identities—signals the most predominant features of your cultural affiliations. Each one of us is made up of the sum total of our cultural identities. We are not a single self, but rather a collection of selves, each one influenced by what we have lived before, what we are living now, and how we hope to live in the future.

A new student enters your classroom, shyly holding out a crumpled piece of paper that appears to be an official school form. Before you reach for the pink slip, you take a moment to study this new person who will share space with you for the rest of the year. Lost in your momentary contemplation, you are startled by the realization that he is studying you just as carefully as you are checking him out. If we could enter both your minds at that moment, we would hear a barrage of internal questions:

Teacher: Well, he looks cooperative enough, but of course, appearances can be deceiving.

Student: Look at her. Giving me the once-over. As if I am some piece of meat she is dying to cut into.

Teacher: What's that tattoo? I wonder if he is part of a gang.

Student:	I can't believe it! This lady is wearing shoes my grand-mother wouldn't even wear.
Teacher:	This little guy could be trouble. I'm going to have to watch him carefully. I think I'll put him in the front, just so I can keep an eye on him.
Student:	She's going to be mean. I can tell already. I bet she puts me in the front so she can watch me every minute.

So goes the kind of internal dialogue in which any two people, including a teacher and a student meeting for the first time, try to size each other up. These first impressions, however distorted and biased based on limited data, help us deal with new interpersonal situations by giving us a starting point for future interactions. They help us to predict behavior so we might protect ourselves if we anticipate trouble. And at least historically speaking, such trouble usually arose from those not-of-our-tribe strangers who looked and behaved differently than what we were accustomed to.

Much of the internal processing that is going on inside us during an introduction to a new student (or any person) is based on preliminary judgments about where this person will fit into our scheme of things. Will this student be a help or a hindrance? Is this kid bright or will she need extra time and energy? What is going to work best to motivate this student and capture her interest? How can I handle this student if she gets out of line?

Although each of the previous questions leads to an answer that can be determined by the student's individual behavior over time, initially we construct hypotheses based on our prior experiences with others who remind us of this particular person. Just as the student is making some assumptions about you based on your dress and various nonverbal cues, so too are you making some initial predictions about what this student may be like. Although it is hoped that both of you will alter your perceptions based more on how you really are as individuals rather than as projected images, much depends on the extent to which you are willing to give the other person the benefit of the doubt.

It is fascinating to consider that no matter how much we attempt to hide or disguise our own cultural origins, other people make assumptions based on limited cues available. How we express ourselves—in vocabulary, syntax, grammar, intonation, and accent—reveals something about where we came from. Our manner of dress, the way we carry ourselves, and physical features related to our size, gender, skin color, hair texture, and facial features, present others with data that they can use to classify us according to cultures with which they have prior experience.

People are thus constantly thinking in terms of culture, trying to make some decisions related to values that matter most to them: Are you like me or different from me? If you give me trouble, how might I protect myself most successfully? Although such prejudgments based on such limited information do lead to misperceptions, prejudices, and other mistakes, such cognitive activity is also quite useful in making predictions about future behavior, especially if perceptions are altered in light of new, updated information.

Part of the teacher's job is to accurately read exactly how to reach each individual student to promote growth and learning. Cultural diagnostics are crucial to forming preliminary plans for how to initiate and respond in many situations. For example, before you discover that Melinda is oversensitive to criticism, that Mikail does not like to be asked to speak out loud, or that Esperanza will answer questions correctly if you prod her several times, you rely first on prior cultural experiences. You know, for example, that among the particular age group and community you are working with (1) boys volunteer more often than girls, (2) Catholic and Mormon children are more prone to approval-seeking than Lutherans, (3) children from the southeast part of the city who are more economically disadvantaged may require more time to complete homework assignments, (4) native Spanish speakers tend to need special help with their spelling to include the silent letter *h*, and (5) children from wealthier neighborhoods may require more structured limit setting because of a sense of entitlement.

These examples are just a few ways that a teacher might establish a set of differential guidelines for students, depending on their *perceived* cultural origins. Obviously, some of these snap prejudgments turn out to be as inaccurate as any other assessment based on limited data, distorted perceptions, and prior experiences that may not generalize to particular situations. That doesn't mean that such assessments are not useful as shortcuts, but they are also potentially inaccurate, given the wide variation in individual differences.

CULTURAL ADAPTABILITY

In your role as teacher, you radiate confidence and authority. You stand before a room full of students utterly in control of yourself and the situation. A few hours later, however, you are in another classroom—this time as a student yourself—and you are tongue-tied, fearful of saying or doing the wrong thing, and concerned that others will find out you are incompetent or stupid. Once again, back at home, you take charge of things again, feeling utterly secure in this culture you have created with your family. Then the phone rings: It is your parents. Once again, you become deferential. You ricochet back and forth all day long from one subculture to another depending on the circumstances and the roles you find yourself in, just as each of your students does. We are all continuously making cultural adaptations according to what is needed.

This ability to adapt to different cultural contexts is the key for many children (and adults) to achieving success in various situations. This is, in fact, the function of culture that helps people accommodate to particular environmental conditions. For example, in Greenland, a culture has evolved that helps its inhabitants to master the challenges related to ice and snow and seals and polar bears. The gang culture of the urban ghetto has similarly evolved as a means by which to help young people survive in the face of poverty, isolation, and ethnic territorial boundaries. Likewise, distinct cultures have developed in every classroom in every school as the norms by which both children and teachers can guide their own behavior and attempt to influence the actions of others.

How well we do our jobs as teachers depends to a great extent on our ability and willingness to help diverse students make necessary adjustments in their behavior from one peer or home culture to a classroom culture, without compromising their essential, prized values. Of course, this also presumes that we can make similar adaptations in our own thinking and behavior according to what is most appropriate.

Disorientation Facing Different Cultures

When we meet a new class, it feels like a first date, with all the accompanying apprehension, nervousness, and excitement. Will they like me? Will I like them? How will we get along? There is a lot at stake because, like it or not, we will be spending every day of the week together in spite of any significant differences in interests or backgrounds.

In the beginning, you feel disoriented, or unsettled, a bit out of control even though you know the feelings wear off—just about the time it takes to adjust to any strange, new culture, whether you are traveling in a foreign country or visiting an ethnic restaurant you have never been to before. At first, you are struck by the strangeness and the differentness of the sights, sounds, and smells. Then you begin to make adjustments as you become more familiar with the place and the people. If you stay there long enough, what initially felt so weird will soon appear quite natural.

After a while, you notice you have learned new words to address people; you appreciate traditional styles of clothing; you are accustomed to sights and smells of different foods, artistic styles, and the instruments and sounds of different music. What was once unfamiliar becomes familiar. Once you get to know the students on an individual basis, your cultural awareness expands further, with greater appreciation for the context of students' behavior. You discover information about their past experiences. No wonder Mia is so defiant given the way she has been so bullied in the past. It makes sense that Trent would appear so quiet and withdrawn considering he is the youngest of nine children. Keisha's annoying disruptions in class seem to reflect the way she gets attention at home. The more you learn about each student, the more their behavior makes sense.

Visiting the homes of your students will give you the opportunity to explore the students' home cultures and learn what skills and resources they bring to the classroom. Perhaps you will discover ways to bring these "funds of knowledge" into the classroom. You will get to know the families on a personal level and strengthen your relationship with the community. A deep understanding of the culture of your students provides a strong foundation for you to build success in the classroom and be able to address difficulties with meaningful interventions when they arise.

Cultures of Schools, Teachers, Classrooms

Ordinarily, we think of culture as it is applied to a person's ethnic background, racial or religious identification, gender, or even socioeconomic class. If *culture* is broadly defined as socially transmitted norms that instill organized patterns of behavior in a particular group, then clearly there are distinct cultures operating in the classroom, as well as in the school itself. There is an assortment of student cultures that play themselves out, easily recognizable by dress, manner, and codes of conduct: jocks, stoners, geeks, slackers, preps, punks, skaters, nerds, and so on. Likewise, there are distinct teacher subcultures in every school: newbies, burnouts, loners, gossips, old-timers, subs, coaches, and others that parallel the various student groups. Each of them represents a tribe of like-minded people who stick together for mutual support or because of shared interests. Such subcultures are inevitable and have been part of human history, yet they are often exclusionary because they are designed to be that way.

School Culture

If we begin with a glimpse into a school's culture, we can find a unique atmosphere prevalent. These norms are established intentionally by both the principal and other administrators through policy statements, staff meetings, supervisory and disciplinary practices, and even in hiring procedures in which administrators are screening for a particular kind of staff contribution. School culture is also influenced to a great extent by contributions from the central district office, which establishes consistent standards across schools and provides professional development. Depending on the principal's style of leadership, delegation of responsibilities, and degree of staff empowerment, teachers also play a big role in creating a school culture. Through their participation in sponsoring clubs, holding after-school tutoring sessions, coaching athletic teams, and interacting with the community, as well as in creating a particular atmosphere in the school through their collective behavior, a school culture emerges. The norms are established implicitly by the behavioral codes evident in the students' and teachers' actions. They are also influenced by a host of other factors—the physical environment, community political realities, regional and neighborhood values, parental preferences, resources available, and historical legacies.

Imagine that we visit two different high schools located in the same urban area. Both are approximately the same size and serve a constituency of children who are from roughly the same socioeconomic background and parallel racial and ethnic representation. Each school, however, has a different cultural climate.

School A received national attention because of its athletic programs. Its baseball teams won the state championship four years in a row. The football and girls' softball teams are dominant in the district. More than half of its golfers and tennis players receive scholarships to Division I universities.

All these athletic accomplishments are proudly displayed as you first walk into the building and see the gleaming trophy case, crowded with honors and tributes accrued over the years. Talk to the principal for any length of time and you will hear him recite the latest in a long series of athletic achievements that occur at his school. This prowess on fields of play is definitely part of this school's culture. It trickles through almost every aspect of daily functioning—the announcements that are read over the public address system, how resources are allocated, the priority for how coaches are hired, and who has the greatest status among both teacher-coaches and student-athletes. This is a distinct culture, one that has many advantages and some side effects.

By contrast, School B has not had its baseball, basketball, or football teams win more than half their games in more than a decade, although its women's field hockey team did advance to the state tournament one year. This is one of the best academic public schools in the city. In one year it had twelve National Merit finalists. Graduates typically attend top universities.

Located in the suburbs, School B has a culture that is regimented and achievement-oriented. The competition is just as fierce as School A—but on a quite different playing field. Here status is determined by class ranking, grade point average, and college aspirations. Obviously, a different school culture prevails, one with its own benefits and limitations. In this case, students care more about grades than athletic scores.

These examples serve not as models but as contrasting cultures that influence what teachers and students do in these environments. Every occupant feels under pressure, in one way or another, to be a particular way, to support a particular goal. Teacher success is judged by different standards, just as student popularity is based on different priorities.

Professional Culture

The norms that have been established by education leaders in the field make up one's professional culture. These include ethical codes for appropriate behavior as well as standards of excellence that most practitioners believe are important. Examples include the development of lesson plans or following a policy of equity in which students of different races, genders, or abilities are given the same opportunities to learn and grow.

Your particular professional culture is also influenced by your level of education and participation in various education organizations as well as professional development opportunities such as workshops and conferences. Those with advanced degrees and those who are often active in local and national teacher associations, would be affected most by these experiences.

Depending on the books you read, the journals you subscribe to, the conferences and workshops you attend, the committees you participate in, the leadership roles you play in the school and community, your professional culture takes a particular shape that best reflects your interests and goals at a given time. This overarching professional identity may or may not be consistent and compatible with the culture of a given school.

One of my (Jeffrey) biggest frustrations teaching in a rural school early in my career was how completely different the expectations, norms, goals, and realities were compared to national standards and what I had been taught in my own training. I would attend regional and national conferences and listen to colleagues talk about issues that had almost no relevance to my life and that of my students back home. The values and outcomes that were discussed at conferences, in journals and books, did not address what we were facing with such limited resources, isolation, and historical legacies.

There is often negotiation involved, both internally and with colleagues, to figure out ways to translate and adapt professional norms and standards to fit the unique demands and limitations of a particular school environment. Depending on the administration, staff, parents, students, and community, all kinds of cultural permutations can develop.

Classroom Culture

Each classroom develops its own culture as well, meaning that each one has its own personality, complete with customs, rituals, language, and traditions. No matter how many years you have been teaching the same grade or subject area it is endlessly fascinating how differently each class develops. You can do the same things, the same way, just as you have for so many years, and yet students respond in unique ways—even when you are positive you are doing basically the same thing.

You have some classes where the students sit silently, rarely contributing unless called upon; in others, you can't get the kids to be quiet no matter what you do. Some classes just don't respond to what you are doing, even though the same approach has worked dozens of times previously. Some groups of students work so well together you are absolutely amazed, while others are constantly bickering and fighting with one another (and with you). Some classes are effortless to teach and others require so much energy you leave feeling exhausted and depleted.

I (Jeffrey) estimate that I have taught a group leadership class over one hundred times in various schools and universities. I am the constant. Over the years, I've developed some rather foolproof and time-tested strategies and exercises that I've refined through so much practice. Yet the main lesson I've learned is that *every* group is different. I tend to get in trouble when I start expecting things to be a certain way or predicting that students will respond in a certain way, just because that's how it worked before. It is interesting how the presence of one particular student can change the whole culture of the class, for better or worse. And it is equally intriguing how we can appear to do the same things, the same way, following the same template and lesson plan, and yet encounter such wild and unpredictable results. I suppose that is one factor that makes teaching so fun and challenging: No matter how long we do this job, how many years we spend in the classroom, how much training we receive or degrees we accrue, or how many books we read, we will never, ever get to the point where we always know what we're doing. It is the distinctive composition of each classroom culture that forces us to reinvent ourselves every semester.

We do our best to build a culture that is most conducive to learning. We hold sacred certain values related to respect, safety, cooperation, and knowledge, and we are quite strategic in setting things up as best we can to reinforce those norms and create a culture that maximizes interaction, curiosity, responsibility, commitment, and so on. We have an illusion of control, at least to start with, in which we are the primary architects of this structure. It is only when construction begins in earnest (usually by the second or third week of classes) that the students forcefully impose their own contributions to this evolving culture. This cocreated project is a living entity, constantly changing as events, crises, critical incidents, and simply normal routines evolve over time.

Classroom culture is created by each teacher in collaboration with the students. Or that's the way it's supposed to work. In reality, it often seems as if it is the students who are the most dominant force in developing particular cultural norms.

WHEN CULTURES COME TOGETHER

What is a teacher to do when the students appear to have so little in common or when they literally do not speak the same language? We live in a country made up of hundreds of different ethnic groups. English is now the minority native language in some schools. Even among supposedly unified groups, there are more differences among various subgroups than similarities. Native Americans are composed of two hundred distinct tribes, and that does not even count the various bands of each tribe, many of which speak separate languages. Hispanics, a coalition of political convenience, include dozens of Latin American countries, each with its own unique set of customs, values, and dialects.

It is inevitable that a teacher, much less any of the students, would have distinct preferences toward some cultures rather than others, especially those that most resemble one's own heritage. Usually biases, prejudices, discrimination, and racism are viewed as a lack of experience, understanding, appreciation, or moral maturity on the part of individuals who develop negative attitudes toward others of a different background.

Because we are not allowed to admit these negative feelings, much less talk about them in an open forum, they often remain underground and unchallenged. They may lead to misunderstanding and conflict. We need to become aware of our preferences and their effects so as to avoid neglect and inflicting harm on others as we work to understand why students behave the way they do. Students may feel undervalued when their cultures are unwittingly misunderstood or policies instituted that are insensitive to their heritage.

One example of this phenomenon occurred in a middle school in a small town in California. A fourteen-year-old Native American child was found to be carrying a pouch with a suspicious-looking substance in it, at the very least composed of tobacco and perhaps even a more illicit drug. The school has a policy of zero tolerance for tobacco or any drug. The student explained the pouch had religious significance to her, that it was given to her by her father to protect her from bad influences. School administrators decided to investigate further, so they cut open the pouch to examine its contents, which, on analysis, were found to be a mixture of tobacco and sage. Consistent with school policy, she was sent home.

Tribal leaders in the area were incensed that she was punished for merely following her cultural heritage. School administrators' attempts to apologize for this misunderstanding did little to mollify what was perceived as assaults to their dignity.

When students do not meet our expectations, our first impulse is to place blame on the offending student(s) as though they are the problem. However, we must step back and ask ourselves, Is there a piece of information that would help us to understand what is happening? Is there a cultural element about which we are ignorant or unaware? While we discuss resolving problems with so-called difficult students in the next chapter, we offer the following situations for consideration, when the teacher is the one creating or exacerbating a problem:

- *The teacher is expecting things the student is unable to do.* Students who have experienced schooling in another country that utilizes oral recitation, such as those in Africa, will not immediately be prepared or comfortable engaging in discussion with critical analysis.
- *The teacher is expecting things the student is unwilling to do.* Sometimes requests of students are made that seem perfectly reasonable to us but are actually quite unacceptable to others. For example, it certainly seems appropriate to ask students to share something they are proud of, unless it goes against their cultural upbringing to "brag" about themselves.
- *The teacher is missing information that is critical to understanding the context for the behavior.* For example, you reach out to touch a fifth-grader reassuringly, but she recoils. You think to yourself that this student is resistant—until you find out later that in her Indonesian culture the head is considered sacred, or in Indian cultures the use of the left hand is avoided.
- *The teacher is subscribing to invalid assumptions.* There are times when you believe you know things that you do not. For example, while there may be a general belief that students of a particular Asian culture excel at school, an individual may have learning difficulties.
- *The teacher is engaging in some activity, technique, or intervention without realizing its implications.* For example, using individual competition in a room where students' cultures value cooperation will likely fail to be motivating.

Culture Clashes

Given the different priorities, values, and agendas of various cultural groups, not only with regard to the ethnicity and religion of the participants in a school, but also among those of the students, teachers, and administration, it is inevitable that there are conflicts. In fact, our educational system is often designed to cater to the preferences of those who are in power to make the rules (school board, administration, teachers, majority culture in the community, legislative bodies, professional leaders) rather than the students who are the recipients of the services.

Let's examine some of the areas of possible incompatibility among these established cultural customs.

Time. The perception of time varies from culture to culture. While schools run on precise schedules, some cultural groups value engaging in relationships over being at a particular place at a specific time.

Assertiveness. Taking individual initiative may be the mark of success in American culture, but it is certainly not part of the cultures to which many Asian children belong. Our schools may value independence, autonomy, and assertiveness, while others emphasize relationships where students are deferential and approval-seeking.

Logic. U.S. schools stress the merits of logic over intuition, thinking over feeling, and deductive reasoning over intuition. In many non-Western cultures, however, quite the opposite is stressed in their value systems. Contemplation is stressed over analysis, which diminishes the essence of a thing.

Written language. Our schools emphasize written discourse over spoken language, especially in most assignments. This agenda is considerably at odds with those cultures that have an oral tradition of language. Among people of Appalachia, Polynesia, or Native American tribes, for example, learning takes place through stories that are passed on from adults to children. Written language is not part of their heritage in the same ways that songs, chants, folk tales, and stories are used.

Spoken language. The language used at home may not match what is used at school. African Americans, Cuban Americans, or Puerto Ricans have dialects of English that are used at home, with peers, and in local neighborhoods. They have their own vocabularies, accents, and traditions.

Parenting roles. In many cultures, families view their responsibility as that of preparing children to come to school, helping children to care for one another, and respecting the teacher. They leave all of the instruction to the teacher while our public schools actively work to involve the parents in the process, a role that some parents are not accustomed to fulfilling.

Don't we already know all this? Isn't this rather obvious?

Of course it is. But we often forget the conflicts students struggle with in the classroom when we interact with them and their families and set expectations for their behavior. Even the topic of homework presents an issue for multigenerational families living in one residence with minimal space for privacy.

We might be tired and annoyed by all the lectures, forced in-service training, and repetitive handouts and articles we are required to read about the critical importance of cultural sensitivity. What sometimes seems lost in the lip service paid to political correctness is that we may forget that *every* student comes from a unique culture, one with its own rules and customs that are at odds with those we hope to establish and maintain in our classrooms.

Incorporate an Anthropologist's Perspective

Margaret Mead advocated as early as the 1920s that training in anthropology should be required for teachers to help them become more flexible and to step outside themselves in an effort to appreciate the experiences of others. She also believed that one of a teacher's primary jobs is to help children make constructive use of their cultural inheritance. An anthropological perspective looks at cultural practices and how community influences a person's behavior.

From such a perspective, the following questions might come to mind:

- What is it about this student's background that leads to this particular behavior and the corresponding underlying meaning?
- What is it that I do not know or understand about this child's background that might help me make sense of what is happening in the classroom?
- How might I investigate further the customs of this child's family?
- What are the interactive effects of having so many cultures represented in this classroom?
- How are my own cultural values and biases getting in the way of honoring those among my students that are different from what I am used to?

We realize that teachers already have enough on our plates without the added responsibility of adjusting what we do to meet the individual preferences of each student, especially when they are at odds with one another. Some students want to work in small groups, others in hands-on applications; some to use media or technology, or hear lectures, or watch videos, or listen to music; others to create something, memorize something, or write something. We try to give a little taste of each strategy, hoping to reach some of the students some of the time.

One stated objective of schooling in the first place is to help diverse children learn a common means by which to work together. But this also presents additional challenges for teachers, especially with increased cultural diversity in our classrooms. That is where adopting an anthropologist's perspective can be so helpful since there is an intrinsic joy and curiosity to the discipline with regard to identifying and understanding patterns of cultural behavior.

I (Jeffrey) was teaching a mixed group of college students recently, using one of my favored and most effective teaching methods—cooperative learning groups. I asked students to repeatedly share with one another in small groups their opinions, attitudes, and personal experiences. Students always love this, at least the students I am used to teaching who are planning for careers in education and helping professions. What I didn't realize, however, is that the engineering, business, and math majors in my class function in cultures in which there are single, right answers. They are evaluated using objective, point systems in which they continually measure their performance. They are never asked to share anything personal about themselves, which would be considered inappropriate, if not intrusive. Yet I was asking them to do things for which they were unprepared and unable to comply. They were frustrated and so was I because I didn't understand their cultures and did not honor them. Instead, I forced them to comply with my agenda, which I believed was good for all people: I tried to "colonize" them. Needless to say, this didn't work very well—for any of us.

It wasn't until halfway through the semester that I took my own advice about thinking like an anthropologist, mostly because it was so obvious that what I was attempting wasn't working. I started soliciting input from the disenfranchised students about what I could do to make the class better matched for them. Some of their suggestions were just not possible, given my teaching style and the content of the class. But I think the most important thing that occurred was that even if I wasn't going to implement a point system of evaluation or resort to lectures with objective exams, I at least listened to their concerns and made minor adjustments in the structure so that what we were doing wasn't quite so radical for them. I still don't think they were happy, but they did feel heard. And I learned a *lot* about challenging my own assumptions about the best ways that students learn.

BECOMING A MORE CULTURALLY RESPONSIVE TEACHER

We liken the path of a teacher as a journey rather than merely a career or a profession because of the endless search for greater competence and proficiency. Experience does not necessarily lead to wisdom or expertise if we don't look for ways to incorporate what we see, feel, and encounter every day into more responsive strategies for reaching a broader range of students.

Cultural responsiveness is one of those attributes that grows more robust with a breadth of life experiences outside of our usual domain. It is one thing to attend workshops and required in-service programs on cultural sensitivity and quite another to immerse ourselves in novel cultures with an open mind and appreciation for "differentness." It is through the fiction we read, the films and media we consume, the conversations we have, and mostly through travel experiences that we broaden our worldviews. That is one reason why the teacher's journey has been designed for periods of reflection and rejuvenation, whether during summers, holidays, or semester breaks.

Certainly we learn a lot through professional training, advanced degrees, and professional literature. Yet greater cultural responsiveness emerges mostly from direct personal experience, especially the kind where you are operating out of your comfort zone, forced to make adaptations to fit in situations where the customs, rituals, and behaviors are markedly different.

We've made a study of how people have forever transformed their lives as a result of cultural immersion experiences while traveling. There are certain change processes that are consistently present, these life-changing events, some of which would be familiar to anyone in the education or helping professions. Many of them have huge implications not only for how we might systematically revitalize our own growth and development but also make significant changes in the ways we teach. It is a sad but accurate reality that when you ask people to share a story of their most powerful and useful learning experiences, almost nobody mentions anything that happened in a classroom (or even in school). More often than not they talk about some struggle they faced in life in which they had to develop or invent or access new resources to overcome the challenge.

Here are some of the most common variables found in such experiences:

- *A mindset ripe for change.* Attitude is everything. As we well know, the mindset that people bring to learning experiences predisposes them to an openness that would not otherwise be possible. Those who go into a situation with an expectation that something wonderful or interesting will happen are much more likely to have those goals met.

- *Insulation from usual influences.* People often report they have come back from an adventure or excursion different than they were before. It is through a degree of isolation, by getting away from their usual routines and influences, that people are more likely to discover something new about themselves or about the world. Imagine, for example, the difference between a trip you take on a bus tour with friends and family accompanying you versus a solo trip you take on your own.

- *Getting lost.* More often than not, the stories people tell of their most transformative travel experiences are those when something occurred that was unforeseen or unexpected. This often involves being lost—actually or figuratively. So it is with those life lessons, or teaching lessons, that we often learn the most from challenges and disappointments when we were way outside our comfort zone and forced to improvise in ways we never imagined.

- *Emotional arousal.* There are high levels of emotional excitement associated with permanent changes, whether in a classroom, travel experience, or any other life event. This can include feelings of joy, elation, and pride, but just as often the experience can involve anxiety, fear, or despair. If you listen closely to people's favorite travel stories, more often than not, they were actually quite traumatic situations in which, only after the fact, they were romanticized and made heroic. The lesson here is that it is during times of greatest discomfort and challenge that the most action is taking place in terms of potential constructive growth.

- *Facing fears.* Growth and learning often come from doing what's most difficult, even if we don't choose these battles; they choose us. Whether during a cultural immersion, leisure or business trip, or just everyday life in the classroom, we are called upon to deal with situations that seem beyond our patience or capability. What doesn't kill us may not always make us stronger (sometimes it is so discouraging we want to quit), but it certainly teaches us things about ourselves, some of which we might not like. It's from facing such fears that we can take ourselves to new levels of understanding or action.

- *Novel experiences.* Related to facing fears and feeling lost, it is primarily the novel experiences that have the most to teach us and stretch us in new ways. We rarely say to ourselves during the moment, "Gee, gosh is this fun, feeling out of control and not knowing what the hell is going on!" Yet once the situation has passed and we have time to reflect on what happened, the learning can become profound. The brain is designed to focus on and remember novel stimuli and situations. Our most indelible memories are often those that presented something we'd never encountered before. It takes a leap of faith, and a certain amount of courage, to remind ourselves when in the midst of a new challenge: "Okay, here it is. This is what I've been waiting for. This is where the action takes place, where I have the opportunity to really stretch myself."

- *Creation of meaning.* One reason it is so important to have trusted colleagues, if not a benevolent mentor, is to have access to a support group to make sense of what you experienced. When you feel sad, disappointed, discouraged, confused, frustrated, overwhelmed, flooded, when as a result of these powerful emotions you are destabilized and at a loss, that is when you need help finding constructive lessons from the experience.

Learning about another culture provides us with information to understand other people's values, attitudes, and behaviors. Learning about families enables us to personalize our interactions with our students. If we can then draw upon their past experiences, skills, and strengths, we will be able to make our teaching relevant and meaningful for them. We can help them make connections to their past and provide background information needed for them to be successful in the future. When we experience what it is like for them to feel lost, not understood, or not valued, we can empathize with them and better anticipate how to meet their needs.

I (Ellen) had a student in my Spanish 1 class who had just moved to the United States from Mexico. She was fluent in speaking Spanish and likely bored in my class much of the time, though her literacy skills were uneven. I noticed she would frequently try to engage the other students in side conversations that were distracting to me and other students. One day when the class was involved in an activity, I went over to talk to her. I mentioned that I thought it must be hard for her to spend the rest of the day where only English was spoken. She smiled and agreed. We talked a bit more. After that day, after making that connection, I noticed she smiled at me more and was rarely disruptive.

Being a teacher is very much like an adventurous journey. Every day brings new challenges, new obstacles to overcome, new tests of our patience and resources. Each day also carries with it the most interesting, exciting, stimulating interactions that help us to feel fulfilled and always learning. Each year we meet new students and their families. Becoming more culturally responsive is about interacting with those who are different and remaining open to their ways of function. It is also about examining critically our own most sacred cultural values and the ways they differentially affect others.

ACTIVITIES AND APPLICATIONS

1. Cultural identity is hardly a singular entity but rather reflects the collection of influences that have shaped who you are. Cultures are reflected not only in race, ethnicity, and religion, but also in a variety of other dimensions including gender, socioeconomic background, age, language, marital status, political affiliation, sexual orientation, geography, physical characteristics, or disabilities. How would you describe your dominant cultural identities that exert the most influence on your own values and interests?

2. Use Google Earth to take a virtual tour of your school's neighborhood community. Better yet, plan a field trip with a colleague to tour local neighborhoods and become familiar with the area.

3. This is a tough question: What are some of the biases and prejudices that you are willing to acknowledge? If *prejudice* represents a prejudgment of people, based on prior experience, then it is impossible not to hold such expectations and opinions.

4. Your students will likely come from dozens of different cultural groups, many of which may be unfamiliar to you. Identify several of the cultural groups that you might investigate further to better prepare yourself to understand the context of your students' experiences.

7

Students Who Drive You Crazy[1]

> *Quick: Who comes to mind when you think about your most challenging students? We are talking about those (hopefully) few individuals who trouble you the most. These are the ones you think about as you drive home after work, as you drift off to sleep at night, or during idle moments when you are not otherwise occupied. Some will haunt you until the day you die.*

Students drive you crazy in many ways. They challenge your authority. They question your competence and have you doing the same. They may be either so disruptive that it's hard to get much done or so withdrawn they seem impervious to anything you could do. They play mind games. Even when they do make progress, they refuse to acknowledge the gains, or at least that you had anything to do with the improvement. They frustrate you to the point that you want to scream, throttle them, or leave education altogether.

AT A LOSS ABOUT WHAT TO DO

The child shows up in front of your desk holding a crumpled-up piece of paper in his fist. He looks vaguely familiar, but he is not one of your regular students. You must have seen him around school somewhere, but you can't remember the context. With a sigh, you figure this is another transfer student,

---

[1] This chapter is based on our book by the same name.

and an impatient one at that: The boy is nervously tapping the chain dangling from his book bag against the side of your desk.

You are tempted to ask him to stop making the annoying sound but decide this is not the best way to begin a new relationship. You put on your best friendly face, with an inviting smile, and ask him to have a seat. He continues standing, increasing the rat-a-tat jangle of the chain.

With a visible show of patience, you ask what he is doing in your room. He flips the scrunched-up piece of pink paper in his hand onto your desk. It slides across the slick surface and lands in your lap. The boy curls his lips into a satisfied smile.

"What's so funny?" you ask him, in a voice that is a little more strident than you intended. It's been a long day, and you can immediately see that you have another challenge to deal with.

Just under his breath, you are almost positive you hear him swear at you.

"Excuse me," you challenge him. "What was that you said?"

"Nothing," the student mumbles. He stares beyond you at the wall as if he is searching for something he lost.

"I'd like you to sit down here for a moment. I think we have some things to discuss." You pause for a moment and then add, "And could you please stop banging that chain?"

The boy looks you right in the eyes, hesitates for a moment, and then shakes his head. "I don't think so."

The student then turns around and walks out of the room, leaving you to stare at the little ball of paper now resting on your desk. Not sure what else to do, you carefully unravel the transfer slip that was filled out by an assistant principal. It reads: "This student has had a schedule change. He will now be in your class." Right.

This challenging student just happens to be of a cultural background different from your own. Interestingly, he is not like this in all of his classes or with all authority figures. In fact, with his music teacher, who is of the same ethnic background as the student, he is one of the most cooperative and motivated students in the class. Clearly, what has transpired between you and the student, as well as between him and a few others, is not only about unacceptable and inappropriate behavior in need of control but also about cultural differences between you. There is a noteworthy absence of understanding that all of the participants in this conflict feel toward one another. Each feels very much like a victim. Furthermore, after this interaction is over, both will receive considerable sympathy from their respective peers as to how misunderstood they have been.

Eye of the Beholder

Although we might agree that this student who swore at the teacher and then stormed out of the room, all without apparent provocation, would be a challenging case for almost anyone, such consensus is not always possible in other cases. In fact, there is sometimes considerable diversity in the opinions of teachers, counselors, and school administrators as to what constitutes a "difficult" student.

Imagine, for example, the following scenario: You intend to present a new unit in class and decide to assess what the students already know about the subject. You ask them to take out a paper and pencil and prepare for a pretest on the lesson. One student raises her hand. You recognize her, puzzled because you see a look of determination on her face. She asks you, politely but firmly, "Why are we doing this?"

How would you interpret this student's behavior?

Of course, this is an unfair question without making other contextual cues available to you—her tone of voice, the previous patterns of her behavior, the responses of her fellow students. Nevertheless, consider your assessment of what you think this question means and how you react, viscerally, to it.

A number of possibilities are articulated by several different teachers:

Teacher A: I think she is challenging me, forcing me to be on the defensive.

Teacher B: She seems to feel a need to exert some control. Maybe she is feeling threatened. She probably didn't do her homework again that day.

Teacher C: I think she's nervous about the test and is trying to think of a way to postpone it.

Teacher D: I like the question. I think that is a reasonable request. If this were me, I would have provided a clearer explanation of what we were doing and why.

Teacher E: 1 wouldn't think anything at all. I don't have enough information to determine what she is really asking. It could mean anything.

Each of these responses is perfectly reasonable. What is most interesting about so-called difficult students is that not everyone agrees who they are. If we get a group of teachers together to describe their most challenging students, we hear quite a variety of nominations:

- "I really struggle with the student who is obviously capable but doesn't apply himself, doesn't study at all, or turn in any work."
- "I don't like the student who always talks back and has to have the last word."
- "I don't like students who are passive, without any opinions of their own. They are teacher-pleasers, always trying to figure out what I want to hear."

- "The student who gives me the most trouble is the one who is manipulative and plays mind games. Everything is about control."
- "I don't like students who are dishonest. I don't mind if they are surly as long as they show how they feel. I have trouble with those who pretend to feel one thing but show me a smoke screen."

Certainly these comments describe familiar characters in our classrooms.

Each of us has struggled, at one time or another, with students who resemble many of these descriptions, just as each of us has encountered individuals like the defiant boy who threw the paper on the desk and walked out of the room. The point is that what constitutes a challenging student is not necessarily the same for all of us. In many cases, it is not just the *students'* behaviors that make them difficult in the first place: It is how *we* react to what they do.

PROFILES OF STUDENTS WHO ARE DIFFICULT

Although it is true that these kids don't really stay up late at night planning ways to make our lives miserable, it sure feels that way sometimes. In truth, they are just doing the best they can with lives that feel very much out of control.

In spite of the differences of opinion among teachers, counselors, and administrators, we can reach some consensus as to which difficult students are cited most frequently. Of course, there are variations in which students are most troubling, depending on their age level. Elementary school teachers and staff face different challenges than those in secondary schools. However, many of the most common examples tend to be those who

- Violate rules
- Lack motivation or interest
- Are deficient in basic social skills
- Carry unrestrained anger and aggression
- Withhold communication
- Appear significantly impaired in cognitive or emotional functioning
- Have many absences
- Are manipulative and controlling
- Push your buttons

It isn't solely the students' behaviors that drive us crazy but also the feelings and reactions that their actions elicit in us. In other words, some students do not just come to us as obstructive or resistant: We make them that way.

Placing Actions in Context

Children are difficult not only because of the ways they act but also because of how we interpret their behavior. Although, as we said, there is some consensus about which children are among the most challenging for teachers, it is worthwhile for us to consider situations from other angles. Keep in mind, as well, that most students (and adults) aren't aware of their motivations for acting the ways they do, nor of the functions that these behaviors serve; they are just doing the best they can to get through the day.

A number of questions might prove helpful in this regard:

- *Who experiences the child as difficult?* It is important to determine who actually "owns" the problem. Does everyone in this student's life experience her as difficult? If not, what might that say about the interactive effect that is going on?
- *How does the child view the situation?* A crucial strategy is to look at things from the other's point of view. In any conflict situation, there are always several different perspectives. You can bet that the child looks at you in much the same way that you view her.
- *How does the child's family view things?* What is their take on the situation? Because everyone is pointing fingers at everyone else as being the source of the difficulty, it is likely that the family will have someone else to blame.
- *How do the child's best friends view things?* This is a *very* interesting source of information. Often when children will not speak for themselves, their closest friends can describe things going on beneath the surface.
- *What precipitates the problem behavior?* What happens just before the problematic behavior arises? What are the situations and circumstances that are most likely to be associated with difficulties? Just as important, what are the exceptions, when the student does not act out?
- *What are the effects of this behavior?* What are the consequences of the student's behavior—not just about the negative effects but also the positive ones? Usually people act the way they do because they enjoy some benefit.
- *What would be the consequences of changing the behavior?* If the student were to change his ways, what would result? Again, it is important to look not only at what would get better but also at what would become worse (perhaps the behavior is a distraction from more serious problems).

- *What are some alternative ways to frame the problem?* What are some different ways in which you might look at things? How could you define the problem in a way that it might be more easily resolved?
- *What is your contribution to the conflict?* This is the most difficult question of all, because it forces you to look at your own behavior and what you might be doing to make matters worse.

These questions can help clarify why particular students seem so difficult to work with. By placing their actions in a context that considers the circular causes and effects, you are able to see more clearly why the behavior is so difficult to change and why these particular students get under your skin.

UNDERSTANDING BEHAVIOR

Before we can ever hope to reach challenging students, we must first understand why they are acting the way they are. All behavior, whether it is comprehensible to you or not, persists because it is helpful in some way to that person: It has some functional value or some protective role in the family. It represents a degree of resilience that allows the student to survive in what is believed to be an unsafe world. Granted, there are negative side effects for the child—and for others—but this may seem like a small price to pay considering the protection that it affords.

They Are Doing the Best They Can

If the child was not getting something out of the behavior, if it was not serving him in some way, he would do something else. Granted, what the child is enjoying may seem mysterious, or even perverse. Nevertheless, all behavioral patterns that continue are being reinforced in some way, if not by friends, then by some inner reward.

An eleven-year-old was referred to me (Jeffrey) as his counselor because he had been caught setting off the fire alarm at school. His parents were puzzled, as were his teachers, because prior to this incident he had been a model student. I spent a few sessions that were most productive with this child. He seemed contrite and cooperative. He acknowledged his wrongdoing and promised never to do anything like that again. His grateful parents called and praised my miraculous work. I must admit that I was feeling pretty good about the work that we'd done.

A few weeks later, the parents called again. I had been so helpful with their eleven-year-old that they wondered if I might be willing to see their eldest son as well. At seventeen, he was a senior in high school and a star on several athletic teams. Lately, his coaches were benching him because of his defiant behavior. This was hurting not only the boy but also the team, which was losing out on his talent.

Again I was surprised at how quickly things proceeded. It took all of three sessions to explore what was going on. The boy admitted he didn't quite know what the problem was, but he was determined to be more cooperative with his coaches. He thanked me for my help and then reported to his parents that he was now much improved.

At this point, I was feeling mightily impressed with myself. Ordinarily, I had never been this successful in such a brief period of time with two children who seemed to be presenting such puzzling problems. Nevertheless, I assumed that my counseling skills were just getting better and better.

When this family called again, asking me if I might see their middle son about some fits of rage he was throwing around the house, I readily agreed. By now, I'm sure that you are nodding your head smugly, seeing the pattern that I had missed—these boys were acting out at school and home for some reason that had to do with their family situation. I must admit that it was weeks later before it occurred to me to work with the parents instead of the children. It took all of five minutes to discover that this couple was on the verge of divorce. I also learned that as long as one of their children was having trouble, they presented a united, helpful front. Once things calmed down, however, then they would both resort to their usual screaming and threatening to walk out. Unconsciously, there was a conspiracy among their children to take turns developing problems as a way to keep the family intact.

In many situations you will see in school, children act out not because they necessarily enjoy being bad, but because their behavior is somehow functional or useful to them or others. Your job will be to figure out what benefits result from their behavior before you can hope to alter the pattern. Even in circumstances when you can't intervene effectively, it still feels better to know that there are legitimate reasons why students appear to act so crazy.

Although the underlying problem in the family mentioned earlier became obvious, in many circumstances it is quite difficult to gather enough information to see the larger picture. For this reason, it is often important to meet with the parents of difficult children so you can not only enlist their support but also read some of what is going on in the family. We are not suggesting that you have either the time or the training to do some form of family intervention, but such explorations will better prepare you to understand what is going on behind the scene.

Applying the systemic model that is now quite popular among therapists, it is assumed that the child's symptoms actually help the family make some organizational transition. Table 1 lists the kinds of situations that you might detect.

Table 1   Home-Life Factors That Can Exacerbate In-School Problems
for Students

Disasters	Transitions
• Natural disasters (hurricanes, earthquakes, fire) • Financial or legal problems • Tragedies (death, victimization)	• Family development (child leaving home) • Individual development • Reorganization following divorce or remarriage
Organizational Disputes	**Hierarchical Disorder**
• Disagreements with school • Problems with community agencies • Distractions from other family problems	• Intrusive grandparents • Unhealthy familial coalitions • Unequal parental power
Discipline	**Marital Conflict**
• Lack of parental consensus • Lack of boundaries and clear rules • Inconsistent enforcement	• Ongoing tension and conflict • Covert battles with children in the middle • Imminent divorce

Challenging students act in ways that appear disruptive, resistant, and noncompliant because of an agenda, often beyond their own awareness, that is fortified by their behavior. Specifically, these students enjoy the following secondary gains from behavior that we label as difficult:

- *The students feel empowered.* If only momentarily, they feel like they are in personal control.
- *The students gain recognition.* They receive the focus of attention at a time when they are unable to be acknowledged for artistic, athletic, academic, or other achievements.
- *The students maintain the status quo.* These behaviors enable them to maintain things as they are, avoid change, or ward off perceived threats.
- *The students get to move around.* Some students have great physical needs to stretch and be in motion at times we would prefer they just sit still.

Additional Functions of Conflict

Given the headaches and heartaches that we normally associate with conflict, whether it is with a student, a colleague, or a family member, we do not often consider how such interpersonal skirmishes provide a number of benefits. These are advantages not only for students who may be the initiators of the disagreement but also for those who exacerbate the problems for reasons of their own:

- *Conflict releases tension.* When tempers are flaring, emotional energy is being expressed. There is an intensity to conflict in which both participants are discharging pent-up feelings.
- *Conflict maintains distance.* Another function that conflict serves is to control just how close one will let others get from a psychological viewpoint. Some children, who are not used to being involved with adults as compassionate and caring as we are, feel vulnerable and confused by their feelings. They have little experience in such healthy relationships and feel unprepared to deal with them.

One of the most effective and efficient ways to push away a well-meaning teacher or other helpful adult is to create some sort of dramatic conflict. For example, I (Jeffrey) recall one four-year-old with whom I had been working to help control her temper tantrums. Every few weeks or so, she would deliberately provoke some argument. She would refuse to abide by the rules we had established. She would do something that she knew would upset me. At first, I wondered why she would deliberately try to do this, until I realized that in her own ingenious way she was keeping me from getting closer to her than she could handle.

- *Conflict highlights issues of control.* In one way or another, conflict usually ends up being about who is going to wield the most power. Disagreements thus signal that both parties are trying their best to exert some sort of command over the other.
- *Conflict underscores underlying issues to be resolved.* Conflicts get our attention. They are disagreeable experiences that churn up a number of negative feelings. As such, they act as motivators to resolve whatever is really disturbing to people.

A teacher was about halfway through a parent conference, going through the usual spiel about how their daughter's low achievement was a reflection more of poor motivation than of lack of ability, when the father and mother erupted into a dispute about whose fault it was that their child was a failure. Interestingly, however, they didn't actually talk about their daughter but rather about whose turn it was to pick up groceries on the way home. The teacher, caught in the middle, felt like he was watching a tennis match, so well rehearsed were their respective "shots" at each other. During an opportune pause in the argument, he offered that perhaps what they were really upset about was how powerless they felt to change their child's behavior. Their conflict only drew attention to the degree of their feelings of helplessness and frustration.

When Biology Has Its Say

Most of what we have been discussing so far implies that difficult students drive you crazy because they are somehow making a choice to be obstructive, resistant, or ornery. It is also important to recognize that a number of children have some recognizable organic disorder. These are children with attention deficit and hyperactivity disorders, obsessive-compulsive disorders, Tourette's syndrome, enuresis, depression, chronic anxiety or panic disorder, autism, schizophrenia, and other progressive neurological disorders. Each of these disorders can result in children's shame, isolation, anger, frustration, and lack of self-control. They all present behavior that is unpredictable, provocative, puzzling, and unmanageable. Furthermore, for every one of these kids, there is likely at least one parent or teacher who blames him- or herself for being unable to exert effective control. Teachers think that parents are the problem. Parents are just as likely to blame teachers. It is this blame and fault-finding that actually prevent us from dealing effectively with the problems.

There are times when it is extremely important to recognize that the problems you are encountering with a student may not be within his control. If you even suspect that such might be the case, you must make a referral to an appropriate medical or mental health specialist to check out the possible organic condition.

Creating Difficult Students

Conflicts in general, and disputes with students who drive you crazy in particular, are almost always the result of some interactive effect in which both parties make some contribution to the problems.

You may be skeptical that this is really the case because it so often seems that you are only doing your job in the best way you know and that some students just seem to enjoy trouble. The interesting thing, however, is that when you talk to these supposed troublemakers, you find that they feel just as misunderstood, unappreciated, and victimized as you do. It is not so much a matter of figuring out who is right, or who is to blame, as it is of simply recognizing that disputes require all participants to make some changes. Most often, you encounter difficulties that are caused (or exacerbated) by your own actions (or inactions) under the following circumstances:

- *When you are missing information.* A student may appear to be unusually reticent and resistant to your best efforts to be helpful. Then you learn that she has been betrayed before by someone she trusted. Furthermore, you learn that one of the messages she received growing up was not to trust anyone in a helping role.

- *When you hold invalid assumptions.* You assume that a child has a problem with authority. After all, in response to your most innocuous requests for compliance, you encounter marked stubbornness. This assumption is challenged after discovering that what appears to be hostility to authority is actually quite a sensible defense against physical and sexual abuse, which she fears at home.

- *When you don't do something very well.* There are times when, as a result of something you say or do, you create difficulties where none previously existed. When you fail to provide adequate structure or clear enough instructions, or when you ask students to do things that are beyond their capability, you create frustration that leads to other, undesirable side effects. When you cut a student off, censure someone, or otherwise show behavior that is perceived as disrespectful, you may have created a difficult student.

- *When you hold an unrealistic expectation.* You expect students to behave in a certain way, to follow certain social norms. Yet your students may have been taught to behave in a different way. You expect your students to call you by your title and last name, yet some students persist in calling you "Teacher." Or you expect students to look you in the eye when you are talking to them, yet they look down. As a result, you feel these students are rude and disrespectful when they are, in reality, following the customs of their culture.

- *When you miscommunicate.* When you misread cues or embarrass a student (even though you had the best of intentions), you may have made an enemy, or at least someone who no longer feels cooperative toward you. Students may not be familiar with words or terms you use, or even gestures. You make a sign with your first finger and thumb closed in a circle to communicate a message of "Okay!" or "Good job!" while this same signal may be interpreted as "You are a zero," or "You are worthless." You may make verbal mistakes in the same way. Expressions you think are positive and encouraging may be sending negative messages that result in students behaving in ways you find disconcerting or inappropriate.

Miscommunications and misunderstandings, in and of themselves, are not necessarily a serious problem—if you have students who feel comfortable telling you when you are off base or when you do or say things that appear to them to be inappropriate. Often our best teachers are our own students.

Multiple Viewpoints

We hear teachers, parents, principals, and counselors say all the time, "I just don't know what's wrong with these kids today. What makes them act so badly?" Of course, in their own discussions when they are left alone, children ask themselves a similar question about adults: "How can they be so stupid and out of it?"

There is a simple answer as to why so-called difficult children act the way they do: It works for them. We may feel angry and indignant because their behavior seems unreasonable and dysfunctional, but that is only because we aren't looking at things from their viewpoint, which is that they are just doing the best they can. If they knew how to do something else that worked better for them, they would do that instead.

Why Students Are Difficult

- They don't know what is expected.
- They lack the skills or ability to do what you want.
- They desire attention, respect, and approval.
- They enjoy exercising power and control.
- They have a low tolerance for frustration.
- Influences at home or in their peer group reinforce their behavior.
- Their physical or psychological safety is threatened.
- They may be victims of trauma or abuse.
- They are bored.
- They have an emotional, neurological, or learning disorder.

Of course, our job is to teach them more socially appropriate alternatives. To do that, however, we must first understand why they act as they do or what they are getting out of those strategies. Second, and just as important, we must examine not only their behaviors, motives, and internal reactions but our own as well. Conflict, after all, usually involves the contributions of two parties who are both acting stubbornly.

PROTECTING YOURSELF

One of the most basic skills we teach beginning counselors and therapists is to adopt a position of neutral detachment in those situations that could become most problematic. We are not suggesting this compromises a level of compassion and caring, just that in some situations, it is important to take a step back. This allows us to disengage from the personal aspects of a conflict and remain clear enough to decide how to respond effectively without being distracted by our feelings of hurt, frustration, disappointment, and anger. It also provides a cushion to help protect us against perceived slights and abuse—that is, if the withdrawal does not become excessively punitive.

Each of us has unresolved issues that are constantly coming to the surface at inopportune times. Most of us actually entered the education field for reasons other than pure altruism. Yes, we enjoy helping people and making the world a better place, but we are also seeking to save ourselves in the process. We want to feel useful and get discouraged when this doesn't work out the way we prefer. We want to be appreciated and pout when this isn't forthcoming the way we would want. We are trying to live up to the expectations of our parents, family, colleagues, and mentors, sometimes feeling like we fall short. Given the personal issues we struggle with, certain buttons are pushed by students who trigger our fears of failure, our secret feelings of incompetence and inadequacy, our feelings of helplessness, our desire for control as well as memories of the most painful times of our own childhood.

During those times when students do or say things that force us to look at our sore spots or to relive unresolved issues related to control, power, intimacy, and authority, we react—or more likely, *over*react—to what is happening. What starts out as a little disagreement becomes a full-fledged battle of the wills.

How Do You Know When a Student Is Driving You Crazy?

This might seem like a rather obvious question, yet, especially when you are struggling with one or two particular students, it helps to get a handle on consistent patterns that give you trouble. The first step is to increase your awareness of the times that you are feeling off balance and upset, conditions that are sometimes denied or disowned in attempts to ward off perceived threats.

How do you know when a student represents a major problem for you?

- When you spend an inordinate amount of time thinking about a particular child or complaining to others about this person
- When you repeatedly find yourself misunderstanding a child and feeling misunderstood yourself
- When you are aware of feeling particularly frustrated, helpless, and blocked with a child
- When your empathy and compassion are compromised and you find it difficult to feel respectful and caring toward a child

Each of these symptoms may signal that you have lost your composure and objectivity. Your own unresolved issues may be getting in the way of being truly helpful to a particular student. Therefore, if we are going to talk about so-called difficult students, we would be negligent if we downplayed our own tendencies to become difficult teachers.

Taking Responsibility

When teachers, counselors, or administrators are stuck, the first place they like to start is with the student. During attempts at consultation or supervision, the professional wants to talk about what the student is doing or not doing or what can be done to change the student's attitudes and behavior. We spend inordinate amounts of time complaining to colleagues, family, and friends about those students who get underneath our skin. There is a challenge common in most staff rooms in which teachers compete with one another over who has the most annoying students, telling stories about the latest atrocities we've suffered or the most dramatic examples of student misconduct. Whereas that does sometimes elicit mild sympathy (if anyone is really listening), it only reinforces a position of helplessness and lack of control.

We have quite a different strategy in mind, one that starts with your own behavior first. Whenever you feel at an impasse in your relationships with students (or anyone else, for that matter), we suggest that you begin by asking yourself the following questions, which represent a summary of issues we have covered previously:

- *What personal issues of yours are being triggered by this encounter?* More likely than not, the student is challenging your sense of competence.
- *What expectations are you demanding of this student?* Often students act out because they are either unwilling or unable to do what you want. It may be time to reassess what you are asking for and make changes in light of what might be more reasonable or realistic.
- *What are you doing to create or exacerbate the problems?* Look at your need for control and the ways you respond when you feel this control is being challenged. Are you pushing this student in ways that are designed to be genuinely helpful to the learner, or are such designs ultimately of more help to you?
- *Who does this challenging child remind you of?* To what extent might you be distorting what is going on with this student? In what ways might you be responding not to who the person really is but to who you imagine the student to be, based on prior experiences with others?

- *Which of your needs are not being met?* It is not pleasant to admit that you have certain personal needs in your work—for example, that students not only learn but also feel grateful to you for your help, that they show appropriate deference, that they confirm your favorite theories about the way people should act, and that they laugh at your jokes.

The intent of questions such as these is to help you to examine thoroughly and honestly your own internal reactions to what is taking place. When you are stuck in a conflicted relationship, rather than blaming the student for being a particular way (about which you can do little), look first at what you might be doing to magnify the difficulties. Change born of self-reflection is actually far easier to effect because it is within your control.

All too often, there is a tendency to pawn off the most difficult students to those who have a reputation for working effectively with the toughest kids. We try to avoid looking at our own responsibility and limitations by referring the problem elsewhere. As tempting as this often seems, we also lose the opportunity to stretch ourselves and develop new skills and competencies that we might otherwise avoid.

In my first year of teaching, I (Ellen) had a streetwise high school student in my current events class. This good-looking, nicely dressed boy was always the last one to arrive in the room, and he had a comment for everything. He didn't think writing, much less spelling, was important. (Later, I would discover that he couldn't read and, naturally, was trying not to let other students know.) In an activity for the whole class that showed misspelling could lead to miscommunication, he finally realized the significance of writing skills. Slowly we engaged in conversation and began to build a relationship. Over time, he became an active participant in the class. At the very end of the year, he would come in the room and ask me if I needed help with anything. I remember what he looked like and sounded like to this day. And it is often the case that teachers report their most memorable students were the most challenging ones.

Recognizing Limitations

No matter how many resources are available to help you with difficult students, there are still limits to what you can do. You are well aware that there are children who are not going to improve no matter what you do, or for that matter, what anyone else may do during your time together. It isn't personal. They live in home environments that are so toxic that they are likely to be scarred for life. They have suffered traumas from which they will need years to recover—far longer than the meager time that you have to work with them. They show the early signs of what are called *personality disorders* (chronic, intractable, self-destructive interpersonal styles) that impair their ability to engage in healthy relationships. Or they are simply stubborn young people who are determined to make life miserable for themselves and anyone else they can capture in their web.

We also have to accept the fact that we just cannot help everyone we would like to, not just because of their limitations but because of our own. Each of us tends to work well with some kinds of people and not so well with others. We all have our sore spots, our areas of weakness. These include deficiencies in our skills. Some of us are better at lecturing or small-group work or one-on-one consultations. One teacher is especially effective in working with passive, withdrawn girls. Another has particular success working with rather raucous groups but struggles with those that are more conventional. Still another teacher works miracles in the classroom when presenting complex content units but bungles inquiry-based lessons that lack structure.

No matter how much we know and can do, or how much experience we have had, we still have to accept the reality that no matter how hard we try, we cannot reach everyone. Under such circumstances, or whenever it appears that a positive outcome is not likely despite our best intentions and more inventive strategies, we would be well advised to work on ourselves as well as our students.

ACTIVITIES AND APPLICATIONS

1. Reflect on the relationships you have with your students. Among those kinds of students who drive teachers crazy, which ones do you consistently struggle with the most? What changes might you implement in the future?

2. Recruit a group of students to meet as a focus group to talk about what teachers do that drive them crazy. Use the input you receive to guide you in the future.

3. In this chapter, there were many different home-life factors that sabotaged students' efforts to do well in school. Growing up, what were some of the challenges that you faced that made things more difficult for you than they needed to be? What could a teacher have done to make things easier for you?

4. We suggested that almost all interpersonal conflicts represent shared responsibility for the problems. Teachers may end up creating or exacerbating problems with particular students because of rigidity, invalid assumptions, missing information, biases, unresolved personal issues, or poor communication skills. What do *you* need to work on in order to become more skilled dealing with challenging students?

8

Stress in a Teacher's Life

> *Stress is one of the most dangerous and insidious forces in daily life. In all its many manifestations, stress increases the risk of dozens of diseases, lowers life span, compromises the quality of life, impairs professional competence, and takes a bite out of your soul. Stress is both the cause of major challenges in a teacher's journey, and also the result of factors that are outside of one's control—limited resources, overcrowded classes, unmotivated students, uninvolved or overinvolved parents, unsupportive colleagues, insensitive administrators. Then there are all the sources of stress in our personal lives once we arrive home.*

Some level of stress is a natural and normal part of a teacher's life, perhaps even an enhancement in mild doses in that it creates drama and excitement, as well as learning opportunities. Stress accompanies any challenge or novel situation. It is the body's way of preparing for such anticipated difficulties by shutting down systems that won't be immediately needed in a perceived emergency (digestion, circulation to extremities, sexual functioning, etc.) just as it revs up those systems that may be useful in battle (heightened sensory acuity, increased heart rate, respiration, etc.). This is all part of the fight-or-flight reflex that was designed to protect us during times of threat. It is indeed the perception of danger that triggers these neurological and endocrine reactions that produce light-headedness, stomach flutters, sweating, heart palpitations, heavy breathing, and so on. When the system is functioning properly, once the perceived threat is reduced, a complementary system turns off the cortisol and other chemicals flooding through the body, returning it to a resting state. The problem is when stress becomes chronic and when the teacher experiences symptoms that interfere with recovery, sleep, and optimal functioning.

SOURCES OF STRESS

It often feels like stress is caused by outside forces, especially those outside of our control. Administrative policies, physical environment, weather, traffic, and especially other people's behavior, are often seen as the culprits that you can hear in the language people use to describe their problems: "The principal makes me so mad." "I can't believe what that kid did today." "If they require one more thing for me to do, I'm going to explode!" "The weather just gets me down."

In some ways, there is a kind of relief assigning blame to external factors, even if it means you are not in control of your own fate. And who is going to argue with you? There are indeed a lot of good reasons for the unnecessary challenges you face, most of which are beyond your control. It turns out that stress in teachers' lives arises from these four main areas:

1. *What others do to you.* Difficult students, incompetent administrators, backbiting colleagues, uncooperative parents, and unsupportive friends or family can all be a source of stress.

2. *What the environment does to you.* The politics, excessive paperwork, conflicted relationships, chaos, negative attitudes around you, and less-than-desirable physical space contribute to stress levels.

3. *What the job does to you.* There is too little time and too much to do. You are on your feet nonstop through the day. Even finding time for a bathroom break is a challenge, much less time to catch your breath. Everyone wants your attention.

4. *What you do to yourself.* Your own unrealistic expectations, fears of failure, self-doubts and insecurities, negative attitudes, and irrational thinking create your own needless suffering.

Interestingly, it is really the last category that you are in a position to do the most about. You cannot make your administrators or colleagues change their behavior, as much as you might like to make that happen. You have far less control over your students' behavior than you would like; you can sometimes force compliance but not cooperation. You are not in a position to alter the economic realities of your district budget or school resources. You have little control over things like the schedule, workload, and class size. You can't even choose the students you teach.

Rather than dwelling on what you cannot do much about, you assuredly *can* deal with the problems you create for yourself. You are in control of your own lifestyle, including the ways you eat, rest, relax, and diversify your life and who you choose to hang out with. You can set realistic expectations for yourself. Just as important, you are in charge of what you think inside your own head and how you choose to look at your situation, even when it is not ideal or what you prefer. You can treat the challenges you face as mere inconveniences and annoying obstacles or you can blow them way out of proportion and totally demoralize yourself. The difference is often a matter of subtleties in the ways you look at your work and your situation.

In the next chapter on preventing burnout, we will talk a lot more about ways to handle challenges and sources of stress; for now, let us peer into the classroom and the mind of one teacher who has managed to stay on top of the stressful challenges she has faced.

Window Into a Classroom

Gwen, a veteran teacher, is late for school, but not because she overslept. In fact, she got up at the crack of dawn so that she could finish grading a stack of papers that students were waiting to receive. It seems that throughout the school year, she felt as though she could never quite catch up with all the demands that were placed upon her by her principal, her department head, her colleagues, the students in her classes, their parents, and her own family and friends. Even the custodian had expectations that she would maintain her classroom in a particular way that was not much to her liking. Sometimes she forgot what she wanted in her own life because she was so used to taking care of everyone else.

Gwen felt that the most important part of her job was to stay fresh and energized when working with children. She tried to demonstrate the creativity and passion for learning that she considered such an important part of her teaching style. The problem for her was how to maintain such a high degree of commitment and excitement for what she was doing when she had six different classes to prepare for each day, over two hundred students to work with, and only fifty-minute blocks of time in which to do it. She also struggled with balancing the need to finish the prescribed curriculum and provide depth of learning as well. Sometimes the curriculum appeared to be a river a mile wide and a half-inch deep.

Furthermore, it was difficult for Gwen to reconcile the requirements of her school district with her actual love of teaching. With the achievement tests, the daily discipline problems, the lack of resources available to her, and the meddling by some administrators and parents, she wondered how any learning took place at all. During those admittedly rare magical days when she felt she had gotten through to her students about something really important, she questioned whether her efforts would ultimately make much of a difference. After all, as soon as the children walk out of her class, they enter the worlds of others who inadvertently or deliberately sabotage her efforts. Not to mention, the children are condemned to serve sentences in the classrooms of some colleagues who, at best, are boring, and at worst, downright incompetent. What the students remember about school was not the fun they had learning in her class, but the abuse they suffered at the hands of others. Then, once out of class, those who really enjoyed learning and took their studies seriously were ridiculed by their peers. Worst of all, so many of the children went home to families that were so deprived or dysfunctional it was a wonder they survived at all.

Gwen considered one student in particular. Dino came from what you might describe as a "conflicted" family. When he was six years old, one of his older brothers killed his younger sister because she would not stop crying. At the time, their mother lay passed out in the bedroom, where she sometimes camped out for days at a time. There was no place at home, or in his whole neighborhood, where Dino could find any privacy for his studies. He could be an outstanding student (and did perform brilliantly during Gwen's class), but he was repeatedly disillusioned by his experiences at home and with several other teachers who were somewhat less than captivating. Lately, Dino had been prone to acting out in Gwen's class as well, so she wondered whether all the time and effort she had devoted to treating him with special care meant anything at all.

EXAMINING THE CHALLENGES

What Gwen enjoyed best about her job was the power she had to influence the growth and learning of young, impressionable minds. This brought her a great sense of pride and accomplishment. What Gwen liked least about her job was the powerlessness she felt in having her efforts repeatedly undermined by influences that were completely out of her control. The struggles that Gwen, the veteran teacher, sought to balance in her journey as a teacher are similar to the challenges facing teachers in schools everywhere, whether they are public or private, urban or rural, at-risk or affluent.

The challenge for teachers is complex. On the one hand, we have a group of professionals who, like most human beings, need to feel in control of their lives; on the other hand, the school environment is often designed (or at least has evolved) in such a way that teachers report feeling so powerless. Since students feel much the same way, the whole atmosphere is permeated with this sense of helplessness. We must realize where and how to focus our attention in realistic ways that have positive outcomes for us.

Real Versus Ideal

In an ideal world, teachers would be greatly appreciated and rewarded appropriately for their worth as the guardians of society's greatest resource—children's impressionable minds. We would have unlimited resources with which to work our wonders and would be able to do so in optimal learning environments that are attractive, stimulating, and comfortable. We would have adequate support in the form of consultants, aides, counselors, and administrators. The parents of our children would be our greatest allies, backing our efforts, magnifying our lessons at home, encouraging their children to be eager consumers of our valuable service. We would have all the resources we desire, state-of-the-art multimedia computers and other technology, books, artifacts, and a wide variety of supplementary materials and supplies.

Most of all, in this ideal world, we would teach students who are eager and highly motivated to learn. They would be well-fed, well-clothed, and well-nurtured at home. They would be polite, cooperative, and well-behaved. They would show us great respect because of our exalted positions as teachers, the imparters of wisdom. Of course, they would be hungry to know everything we have to offer and yet still beg us for more. Discipline would certainly not be a problem, because they would view the opportunity to attend school as a privilege.

Furthermore, central administration and our own principal would have utmost trust in our competence. Money would be available for all the in-service training, supervision, and professional development that we could desire. Paperwork, lesson plans, self-evaluations, and annual reviews would be kept to a minimum, so that we could do what teachers do best—help children learn.

Well, you only have to compare this ideal world of education to that of everyday schooling to get a gigantic dose of reality. That is why so many teachers struggle with confronting their own sense of powerlessness. Once upon a time, they felt sure they could set the world on fire, just like you. Then they faced the realities of teaching. Many of their children were so underprivileged, unmotivated, disadvantaged, and distracted that performing well in school was their absolute last priority. Not infrequently, teachers feel completely at a loss as to what to do when they stand in front of a class where students are bickering and throwing things across the room, while the best-behaved ones are withdrawn and maybe even dozing with heads down at their desks. Then, if by some miracle these teachers can attract and maintain the students' attention, how are they to communicate when the students either do not speak English or have limited English proficiency skills? How do they meet the needs of individual students with varying special needs? How do they make personal connections when there are over forty students in a classroom and not even enough seats to go around? And what happens after the class is over? What is the likelihood that the students will do any homework or study for the next day? How will they ever prepare students for all the mandated achievement tests when many lack the prerequisite skills and knowledge expected of students at their grade levels? The good news is teachers do not have to answer all these questions simultaneously. They acknowledge the areas in which they have control, set goals, seek answers, and address issues as they arise to the best of their ability with support from colleagues and mentors.

For those who were impressed initially with the supposed short workday and school-year calendar, the reality turns out to be something quite different. Parent conferences and Individualized Education Plan (IEP) meetings may occur before or after school or during a preparation period. Department meetings, faculty meetings, and district curriculum meetings are generally held after school. Professional development programs, while often held during the day with released time provided by a substitute, are also offered after school and during the summer so teachers won't have to leave their classes. Teachers need time to consult with colleagues to improve their practice and continually upgrade technology skills. Additionally, new teachers go through induction programs generally for the first two years. Veteran teachers often become mentors or supervising teachers for university student teachers, which requires extra thought and time. Teachers are constantly asked to lead after-school programs for remediation, sponsor clubs, or coach sports. Evening programs include "Back to School Night," "Open House," and "Family Nights" for mathematics, science, history, geography, or other subjects. While the timing is flexible, teachers grade papers, prepare lessons, request supplies, and complete progress reports "after" school or on the weekends. As a result, successful teachers carefully plan their calendars and guard their schedules so as not to commit themselves to the point that they feel overwhelmed with obligations. Unfortunately, stress is often a constant companion.

We don't mean to be unduly discouraging for those of you who are beginning your careers, or in any way to temper your enthusiasm about doing things differently; we just want to acknowledge the sources of stress before we discuss what to do about them. For every burned-out, despondent teacher who feels powerless, there is another one who has developed the inner resources to retain a sense of potency, even in the face of annoying and inconvenient alterations. They know new programs will be identified as "the remedy," instituted and then discarded when deemed inappropriate later. New administrators will bring ideas and programs that worked in other places to try with your population. In fact, these teachers even prefer to consider these ongoing situations simply as challenges that can be overcome with a little patience, fortitude, and ingenuity.

Yes, it would be wonderful to work in a school where you are empowered by the principal, the parents, and the system to work effectively as a teacher. Suppose, however, that you are not one of these fortunate ones. Moreover, let us assume that your work environment is fraught with obstacles and is sometimes downright hostile. In the section that follows, we share some strategies you can employ to help you maintain your idealism and enthusiasm for teaching and learning even in such a challenging environment.

Succeeding in Spite of Stress

Ray is respected by his high school colleagues, as well as the student grapevine, as being a competent, dedicated teacher. His students describe him as a "together guy" who "really cares about us as people." In spite of his well-deserved reputation, Ray gets little support from the administration in his impossible assignment of making competent, sensitive writers out of his 150 students. In fact, the principal observes him for about fifteen minutes a year; gives him a swift, superficial evaluation; and praises him for maintaining effective control of his students. The principal rarely makes any acknowledgment of the fact that Ray is an extraordinary teacher.

What are the sources for Ray's success as a teacher? One of the factors is revealed in the assessment his students give of him. He possesses a strong identity built on a genuine feeling of self-worth. He has learned that his true identity is built on a number of self-images: husband, father, friend, teacher, writer, poet, individual, and risk taker. He recognizes that he continues to evolve based on the new experiences, new people, and new places he encounters in his life.

Although Ray recognizes these new images of his dynamic, developing identity, he also takes comfort in an inner core of his being that remains grounded. This inner core provides Ray with a personal meaning that empowers him as a satisfied, integral person. At one time in his life, he searched outside of himself for peace, happiness, and joy. His search ended, after much personal pain and despair, when he found he had the power to find the peace, joy, and happiness he longed for within his own being.

Ray is a fully functioning human being who knows how to flex his individual self to accommodate the rigid demands of the environment in which he lives and works. This flexibility provides him with a subtle but conscious control over many aspects of his workaday world. He may bend, but he does not break.

Ray sets reasonable goals and takes pride in what he is able to accomplish in the classroom. He carefully builds relationships with students throughout the year, recognizing that this process takes time and effort. He works to establish a comfortable environment in the classroom where his students will feel safe asking questions by providing them opportunities to get to know one another in risk-free ways. He has them take time to interview one another, and he has them work in small groups to complete structured tasks. He is quick to end any form of harassment such as ridicule. He asks his students to share their writing with one another, and he also reads them examples of his own work. He praises them for their achievements and helps them to recognize the progress they make throughout the year. He would like to reach all students, but he knows some will be beyond his grasp.

By peering into Ray's classroom or chatting with him in the hallway, you might very well get the impression that he is a fairly laid-back, relaxed guy who is in complete charge of his world. You probably know people who seem very much like him. But make no mistake: Ray has struggled with tremendous stress in his personal and professional life. What may appear easy and effortless is a constant battle for him, especially considering a history of some fairly dysfunctional behavior in his past.

Maladaptive Coping Strategies

Prior to reaching a state of relative peace and tranquility, Ray struggled with stress in a multitude of ways, relying on some coping strategies that, while common, are not particularly effective. As you review each of these popular but maladaptive choices, consider their possible relevance to your own life or to others you may know:

- *Ignore the problem and hope it will go away.* This is almost always the first choice when facing difficult situations that require considerable effort. You aren't sleeping well, or feel agitated, or can't stop ruminating about something bothering you. Just try to shrug it off and hope things work out on their own or the problem just magically disappears. This isn't a bad first alternative—wait and see what happens. But if nothing changes or things become worse, waiting longer isn't helpful.
- *Complain and blame.* This strategy elicits sympathy and self-pity. That feels good for a little while, as does the belief that the problem isn't your fault. But it doesn't help you to actually do anything constructive to resolve the stressful situation.
- *Isolate.* When you are feeling vulnerable or hurting, it makes sense that you want to protect yourself and lick your wounds without risk that anyone will make things worse. This can be a desirable first step when under extraordinary stress, but ultimately isolation can lead to more severe loneliness, depression, and helplessness.
- *Self-medicate.* If there is a pill you can take, or some behavior that will temporarily alleviate the pain, that is a very seductive option. All kinds of addictions and habits begin not as pleasure-seeking

activities but rather as attempts to reduce discomfort. Alcohol, prescription medications, and illicit drugs are obvious examples—and they *do* work, even if they have significant side effects.

- *Engage in emotional eating.* If the goal is to soothe pain and moderate stress, indulgences like overeating and other behavioral habits work well in the short run. The same is true for those who escape in media, spending hours every day lost in television, videos, online porn, social media, and games. Each of them does provide temporary relief in the form of escape, but ultimately doesn't address the source of the stress or provide a constructive and, therefore, more effective and lasting solution.

STRATEGIES FOR REDUCING STRESS

If the methods just mentioned only work in the short run, or have undesirable side effects, what are the best alternatives for dealing with stress? We'll talk more about self-care in the next chapter, but these are some of the most effective options:

➤ *Reframe the concept of stress.* Stress isn't necessarily a bad thing. There are actually three different forms of the condition (*stress, neustress, which is neutral has no good or bad effects,* and *eustress, which stimulates us in positive ways*), the last two of which can actually *enhance* performance. In moderate or minimal doses, during brief intervals, stress produces heightened sensitivity and acuity. Stress is another way of describing excitement, which can be enjoyable (or at least tolerable) if it dissipates after the incident. People deliberately seek out risk-taking, adventurous, and exhilarating experiences that are specifically designed to jack up the nervous system. It often helps to remind yourself that stress, in itself, can perform important roles in focusing your attention on unresolved issues and the tasks ahead.

➤ *Examine secondary gains.* Stress that is chronic, unremitting, and overwhelming sticks around for a reason. Ask yourself what you have been ignoring, what issues you have been avoiding, what business you have put aside. Many negative emotions are actually designed to make you miserable enough that you will make needed changes. Stress also serves important functions, as well as those that are counterproductive. What are the benefits or secondary gains from stress? You get attention. You get to feel like a victim. You have an excuse for avoiding things you don't want to address: "I wish I could do that job, but right now I'm just not feeling well."

➤ *Breathe.* The respiratory system is one of the first areas affected by stress: breathing becomes shallow and rapid, without providing sufficient replenishment of oxygen. Almost every activity designed to reduce stress (meditation, yoga, tai chi, chanting, exercise) involves breath work of some kind. Among all the strategies for reducing stress there is almost none more immediately effective than simply concentrating more fully and completely on your breathing. During times of crisis, when faced with difficult challenges, when feeling out of control, taking several deep, deliberate breaths provides almost instant relief.

➤ *Practice relaxation-training techniques.* Visual imagery is often used to systematically relax most of the muscle groups. As you are probably aware, stress is not just an emotional response but one that is experienced in many parts of your body. Shoulders become tense. Teeth clench. Pain settles in the lower back. Fingers and toes feel tingly. Headaches, stomachaches, joint pain, and other maladies are common reactions. Relaxation training teaches you to combine focused breathing with images of your muscles unwinding, stretching, and soothing themselves. Beginning with the tips of your toes, to the top of your scalp, picture each muscle relaxing until all stress is banished.

➤ *Be assertive.* Sometimes stress results from interpersonal conflicts in which your rights have been compromised. This can involve students, colleagues, administrators, or anyone else in your life. The two extreme positions in such a circumstance are to overreact through inappropriate aggression, or underreact through avoidance and passivity. Being assertive represents a middle position in which you stand up for your rights but do so in a respectful, sensitive manner. This is, of course, really hard to do when you feel threatened or abused in some way.

➤ *Seek support from friends.* Assuming that the source of stress doesn't originate from friends, soliciting support from others is immeasurably helpful, especially if they are good listeners. Even if you must suffer for a period of time, it is much easier to do so when you're not alone.

➤ *Self-talk.* This is the bread and butter of all forms of self-help, especially when dealing with stress. It involves monitoring carefully what you are telling yourself inside your head about what's going on and then changing the negative feelings by altering the internal dialogue. Compare the difference between "I can't believe they are *doing this to me*" and "I can't believe *I am allowing this* to get to me." Self-talk involves challenging those thoughts that are not based in reality, or represent exaggerations and distortions, and instead substituting more clear and logical statements.

➤ *Keep a stress journal.* It helps to keep track of what most frequently gets underneath your skin in order to identify patterns. One template involves simply dividing a sheet of paper into columns to describe what happened, when and where the incident occurred, who it involved, how you felt, and how you reacted. It feels good just knowing that you are doing something constructive to monitor your reactions, even before you develop any plan for intervention.

➤ *Disconnect.* This might seem like a contradiction to the previous suggestion about seeking support from others, but one major source of stress is the constant intrusions that come from phones, computers, and other mobile devices. There is virtually no downtime anymore. You see students (and teachers) texting every hour of the day. Everyone has a phone or related device glued to his or her ear. It's hard to get much done with the constant interruptions from e-mails, texts, and calls. One way to insulate yourself from additional stressors is to make a conscious decision to turn your devices off for periods of time, to leave your phone behind, to turn off the settings that interrupt your daily activities. Access technology on your own terms rather than when others want access to you.

➤ *Constructively escape.* We mentioned maladaptive forms of escape earlier, those that have negative side effects or are taken to extremes. Yet it's critical to develop consistent ways that you can relax, recover, and just check out for a period of time. That can involve hobbies, movies, books, video games, social media, or just solitude—but all in moderation and in controlled doses.

➤ *Exercise.* Stress interferes with sleep as well as the ability to concentrate. There is no better way to burn off excess energy and help yourself to relax than following a consistent exercise program. You know this. Everyone knows this. But relatively few teachers follow through with this commitment on a daily basis—with lots of very good reasons.

➤ *Slow down.* In the hurried, frantic universe of a teacher, it takes conscious effort to slow down. *Flow* is the term coined to describe the meditative-like concentration on everyday activities—deliberately slowing down and focusing on every task to reduce stress and increase enjoyment. We sprint through our lives, moving from one thing to another without real appreciation (or even awareness) of the task. Stress is often reduced by taking the time to really focus on the most ordinary behaviors—slowing down the pace of eating, walking, anything that helps you live more in the present moment.

➤ *Get help.* When stress runs rampant, when you feel out of control or experience major symptoms that disrupt the quality of your life, it is time to ask for help. Ask a friend, or the school counselor, for a referral to help you deal with the issues that are getting in your way.

Change Is Difficult

So you think you have heard this before? We agree. You *have* heard most of these suggestions before. How many times has someone told you that it's a good idea to eat more healthfully, lose weight, continue an exercise program, or reduce the stress in your life? So the big question is—Why is it so difficult to put any of this into practice in any sort of permanent way?

We've already discussed some of the "benefits" or secondary gains of remaining stuck. The great thing about being stressed, and staying that way, is that you have a ready excuse for not performing at the highest level ("Hey, I can't help it. You can see how busy I am"). You get to feel like a victim and elicit sympathy from others ("I'm doing the best I can, but you can see how I'm suffering"). You can blame others or things outside your control for your plight ("It's not my fault"). And as long as you stay frantically busy and overstressed you can distract yourself from other things you'd rather avoid examining (boredom, loneliness, isolation, feelings of failure, family problems). All in all, stress often sticks around because it is useful to you in some way, even with the collateral damage it causes to your health and psyche.

Even when you do feel a certain commitment to take constructive steps to reduce stress, the behaviors don't become sufficiently habituated. After all, you don't make a decision each morning about whether or not to brush your teeth—you just do it because it is part of your normal routine. You don't decide if you are going to check your e-mail or messages every day—it's just what you do automatically. So it is with any lifestyle change you wish to initiate, whether it is exercising every day or slowing down the pace of your life: You must make these daily habits that you do without having to make a conscious decision.

Change efforts are also sabotaged by negative self-talk when you say things to yourself like, "This probably won't work"; "Because things didn't work this time, they'll probably never work now"; "I can't stand this situation any longer"; "This is terrible that I didn't get what I wanted"; "Nobody really cares about this anyway." It is inevitable that attempts to make any change in your life (or help others to make such changes) will result in occasional relapses and setbacks. It is important to be realistic about what you can do and the time line that is reasonable to accomplish your goals. It is also critical to take things in small, incremental steps that slowly build on what you've begun earlier.

Remember Why You're Doing This Work

The stress and challenges you face are the logical consequences of your chosen profession. It would be senseless for someone to complain that a roller coaster is scary, a hiking trip is tiring, or a traveling adventure is sometimes a bit risky—that is exactly what is to be expected from the experience. Likewise, a teacher's journey is one that is fraught with challenges and a certain amount of stress; it comes with the territory. But remember why you decided to become a teacher in the first place, as some of these statements capture the motives:

- *I love children. I've always liked being around kids. In fact, I feel more comfortable around them than I do most adults.*
- *When I was struggling as a kid, one of my teachers was really there for me. She listened and supported me when nobody else believed in me. I want to pay her back by helping others like me.*
- *I get a kick out of seeing people do new things on their own. It feels like such a privilege that I can be part of that growth.*
- *What I do best in this life is learn. I'm captivated by learning. It is natural for me to want to model what I do best for my students!*
- *There are lots of callings in life, but none, I believe, as high as the profession of a teacher.*
- *I want to make a difference in the world. I want to feel that I have helped to make things better.*

It is this last statement that is at the heart of most teachers' motives. There is a wonderful feeling of satisfaction in knowing that you have made a difference in someone's life, that if it were not for your efforts, a small part of the world would be worse off. It is the power to influence others that is so attractive to many of us who choose to be teachers. We giggle at the prospect of introducing some novel idea to children that we just know will change the way they see themselves or others. We feel dizzy with glee after getting through to someone who had previously been unreachable.

Exemplary educators are not motivated by external rewards, nor by the hunger for power and prestige. Rather, most often they describe the ways they have been able to express their creativity and autonomy in the classroom. They prize their meaningful relationships with students and colleagues. Most of all, they *know* they are making a difference in young people's lives. Sure, we pay a price for our commitment to help others. Yes, we are overworked, underpaid, and often unappreciated. We face a number of challenges that are outside of our control. We confront students who are rude and defiant, as well as parents who are aggressive, misguided, or unavailable. We are under continuous pressure to meet external standards that we may not embrace. We feel administrators do not support our work. Stress is ever present and sometimes feels unmanageable.

Teachers who are most fulfilled and satisfied in their work are those who have discovered ways to meet the challenges they face with optimistic, yet realistic, expectations. They focus on what is within their power to change rather than harp on those factors that are outside their control. They have taught themselves to live with stress in such a way that they can keep negative symptoms to a minimum as well as appreciate the accompanying excitement as a normal part of the journey.

ACTIVITIES AND APPLICATIONS

1. What is the greatest source of stress in your life right now? What do you identify as the cause of this stress, and what is within your power to change?

2. Talk to several teachers whom you perceive as remarkably skilled at handling stress that arises. Seek out those who always appear to remain calm and in control, regardless of the situation. Find out how they maintain this equanimity.

3. Reflect on the various measures you currently use to alleviate stress. Are they maladaptive or effective strategies? Which ones will help you realize your potential in light of demands placed on teachers today?

4. As you will recall, eustress is the kind of stress that actually enhances performance and enjoyment because of the excitement it generates without lasting negative side effects. All the drama associated with teaching can indeed become a source of tension, but also of joy, depending on how it is framed. Think of an example in which others have become extremely upset about a situation that you were able to keep in perspective, and perhaps whose drama you could even enjoy.

9

Self-Care

Avoiding Burnout and Rustout

> *Two teachers are leaving the school building after a long day. One looks haggard, his features drawn, his posture stooped. He shuffles toward his car carrying a huge backpack filled with books and materials. He stops for a minute to catch his breath, rearranges the straps of the heavy bag, and then continues onward with a deep sigh, as if he is not sure he wants to take another step forward but certainly has no desire to go back where he came from.*
>
> *By contrast, the second teacher has a definite spring to her step. Once she says goodbye to her dispirited colleague, she practically breaks out in a spontaneous skip. She is more than ten years older than her fellow teacher but looks quite a bit younger. She, too, stops for a moment, but as she looks over her shoulder back at the school, she starts to smile, remembering what happened during the day.*

How is it that two teachers who do pretty much the same job, sharing identical responsibilities and working with the same population of students, can react so differently to what they have experienced? The first teacher leaves each day feeling utterly exhausted and run down. When he returns the next morning, he will still be operating with the emotional and physical deficit that has been accumulating for years. The second teacher, however, feels absolutely invigorated as she launches herself out of school into her world. She feels great about what happened during her day and just as good about what is waiting for her at home. She will reenergize and have a smile on her face when she returns the next day.

As we've seen in the previous chapter, the ways that teachers tend to deal with the challenges they face and metabolize the stresses they encounter depend on a number of factors. Some teachers, like the first one, seem unable to manage their workload and find it difficult to set and enforce limits on other people's demands of them. They are often discouraged and demoralized, sometimes even embittered. They are not much fun for their friends and family, and especially their students, to be around. Other teachers seem to find ways to take things in stride, to immunize themselves against the inevitable toxic elements that inhabit schools. They not only meet challenges that others find daunting but even flourish because of them. Which teacher would *you* like to be?

AN OCCUPATIONAL HAZARD

In almost every people-oriented profession, from medicine to law enforcement, from social work to teaching, you will find a common malady with universal symptoms suffered by these diverse practitioners. Maslach (1982) described *burnout* as a professional hazard characterized by the following eight symptoms:

1. A reluctance to discuss one's work with others

2. A high incidence of escapist daydreaming

3. Attitudes of cynicism, negativity, and callousness toward one's clients

4. Loss of enthusiasm for work

5. Emotional exhaustion and feelings of being used up

6. Decreased effectiveness in job performance

7. Blaming others for one's current unhappiness

8. Feeling powerless to alter one's situation

Burnout is a form of occupational stress that is an inevitable struggle for all helping professionals who work with others, no matter how dedicated, committed, and skillful they may be. It is a condition of emotional depletion, one in which satisfaction is significantly reduced, as highlighted by this disclosure:

I look at the kids today and I can only shake my head. I don't know what happened to this generation but—and excuse my language— they just don't seem to give a shit. It's hard for me to care much about whether they learn anything or not because they don't seem to care. Their parents don't care—or else they care too damn much, always

*telling me how they think I should do my job. Don't get me started—
but these new teachers coming out of school aren't much better. They
think they know it all, but let me tell you, they don't have a clue. They
come here all starry-eyed like they're going to actually change the
world or something. Hah! They'll find out soon enough.*

From your perspective right now, filled as you (hopefully) are with
excitement and enthusiasm for the profession of teaching (otherwise, why
would you be reading this book?), you may feel reluctant to admit you
would surrender to listlessness and despondency. It would also be nice if
you didn't have to run into a teacher like the one above who has completely
given in to his feelings of despair. As much as you may be telling yourself
that you are immune to these feelings, that this would never happen to you,
we have some disappointing news: It is inevitable that sometime during
your journey, there will be times that you feel demoralized and discouraged,
although we expect this will be a transitory period that you will eventually
come through with even greater resources and renewed commitment.

I (Jeffrey) have quit more teaching jobs then I would care to admit,
all for slightly different reasons that are really just variations of the same
themes. I get bored easily. I can't abide bullies and hate people trying to
control me or tell me what to do. I get tired telling my same old stories,
doing the same things the same way. I don't like being around people who
are mean to one another. As I review the list of reasons (excuses?) I've abandoned jobs, I realize that almost none of the changes I made had anything
to do with the students. I've always *loved* my students, regardless of their
age range (from preschool, elementary and secondary school, college-age,
master's, and doctoral students). I've almost always enjoyed the settings of
the schools (urban and rural, inner city and suburban, academically demanding and rudimentary, American, South American, Asian, South Pacific,
European, even Greenlandic). I've liked the variety of teaching assignments
and especially the ongoing relationships with students.

So, what's the problem, you ask? Usually the major source of my frustration and burnout comes from supervisors or colleagues who are not supportive (or don't feel supportive enough). I flee teaching assignments when
I don't have the kind of collaboration and cooperation that drew me to the
profession in the first place. It's taken me years, decades actually, to develop
the internal resources and coping skills so that now I have the capacity to
find or create satisfaction without having to switch jobs as burnout sets in.

Although we have been speaking about this condition of burnout as
something that happens to you all of a sudden, it is more accurately an
insidious, progressive form of self-neglect. In its worst state, it represents
a kind of slow deterioration that eventually rusts and corrodes the edges of
your compassion and caring.

Last year, Amanda was in the middle of her third year of teaching. If you had dropped into her fifth-grade classroom, you wouldn't have guessed that she was still a relatively new teacher.

She did not struggle, as many rookie teachers do, to control disruptive students. Amanda was not disturbed when the principal popped in unexpectedly to conduct his annual evaluation of her teaching. Her bulletin boards were filled with colorful illustrations; her walls were lined with examples of outstanding student work. Had you taken a quick look at her lesson plan book, you would have been impressed to find that she was not just slightly ahead in her planning—she had completed her lessons for the entire school year.

This window into Amanda's classroom one year ago might present the picture of a fulfilled teacher—that is, if you did not look very closely. The fact is, as Amanda later admitted, she was exhibiting the signs of a form of burnout that Gmelch (1983) described as rustout.

Rustout is a type of burnout that afflicts teachers when they temporarily or permanently cease to be enthusiastic learners. The excitement of learning is what first attracted many teachers like Amanda to the classroom. Learning provides the joy, delight, and wonder that leaves little room for boredom or boring routines. Learning sustains interest, promotes risk-taking, and rewards the teacher with the energy required to continue the hard work of exploring, searching, stretching, inventing, constructing, and so on.

If you had observed more carefully Amanda's classroom last year, you would have come to recognize the clear evidence of the onset of her professional rusting out. Look at those bulletin boards again. Sure, they are colorful, but they are also laminated to childproof them and preserve them for next year's use. These flower-filled spring scenes decorate the room, but they do not invite her students to use them as tools for learning. There is virtually no evidence of technology use in the room because Amanda hasn't had the time or interest in adapting what she's been doing to other modalities.

Check out her examples of high-quality student work that line the walls. The writing samples are error free but bear a striking resemblance to one another. They show no evidence of the impishly delightful senses of humor of fifth-grade students. Not one piece of writing rings with the authentic voice of a vibrant child. The lesson plans, so dutifully prepared for the entire year, provide another piece of evidence of the rigid, risk-avoiding environment that paralyzes the learning of Amanda's students. She was no longer an effective model of learning. She was cruising the class on automatic pilot. Although she appeared to be efficiently moving her students from Grade 5 to Grade 6, the magic was gone. Amanda was an unknowing victim of rustout.

That was last year. This year, at the beginning of the second semester, Amanda's deadly routine was abruptly changed when she was requested to supervise a student teacher. Maryann came into Amanda's class in January, filled with a vision of limitless learning opportunities for her first class of real fifth-grade students.

Maryann made the mistakes any beginning teacher would make and agonized over them but learned to get back on track. She kept one step ahead of her students and frequently found ways of using their diversions as paths to unplanned but powerful learning.

For science, Maryann took her students outside to an adjacent area, staked out a four by six foot plot for each student, and showed them how to observe and describe the conditions of the soil, weeds, and insects of each student's piece of ground. During the semester, the student inspected his or her piece of earth weekly, measuring the growth of plants, noting the effects of pollution, and sharing concern about people's insensitivity to the care of the earth.

Maryann's bulletin boards were interactive centers where students learned to create limericks, solve mathematical story problems, and fill out question-naires about issues vital to fifth-graders. She displayed many samples of her students' writing, most of them works in progress, such as the letters each was writing to a favorite author. There were no paint-by-the-numbers kinds of student work. Maryann had taken the time to discover the multiple abilities of all her students. Their artwork and poems, their recipes and story problems, their blogging sites revealed the unique gifts of culturally diverse children.

Maryann revealed another admirable quality of a genuine teacher—she stayed consistently and consciously on the learning curve. She learned from those peers who were eager to share the wonder of their professional lives with her. She learned from sharing her highs and lows each evening with her husband. From her master teacher, Amanda, she learned how to consult with parents and to organize students for tasks, such as food collections, picture taking, and fire drills. Maryann consciously learned from her students, who eagerly shared their unique skills, hobbies, and experiences with her and with their classmates. Some of the students came from wealthy families; they shared experiences and artifacts collected on vacations to Washington, DC, Paris, and New York City. Other students were the sons and daughters of migrant farm workers. They shared stories and mementos from their travels to the cotton fields of Texas, the vineyards of California, and the orchards of Oregon.

Most of all, however, Maryann learned from trial and error. Her mistakes were not sources of shame; they were challenges to construct new learning approaches. She learned to trust her instincts about her students' growth. She learned about her own values and how to affirm them without unduly influencing the beliefs of her peers or her students. She learned her limits, but she also learned to constantly test these boundaries. She learned that neither she nor her students were perfect, but she recognized that they did not have to settle for mediocrity. She daily challenged herself and others to strive for excellence. Most of all, she learned that the major source of rewards for her hard work as a teacher came from belonging to a community of lifelong learners who genuinely care about one another:

Needless to say, Maryann's student teaching was highly successful. It provided her with the guided practice and feedback she needed to successfully launch her career in teaching. It also created a turning point in the career of her master teacher, Amanda, who was unconsciously in the grip of professional rustout: "I never expected that a student teacher would make learning fun for me again. I can't wait to get my students back and start over again."

Starting over again is what Amanda realized she must consciously do at the beginning of each school year to avoid the stultifying effects of rustout. The powerful daily demonstrations of genuine learning orchestrated by her enthusiastic

student teacher had so transformed Amanda's students from reluctant partici-
pants to eager learners that Amanda was convinced that she had to change.
Maryann's daily modeling of student-centered learning also gave Amanda the
potent remedy she needed to counteract burnout and rustout and to transform her
future classrooms into laboratories for student learning.

The paradigm shift Amanda made in her professional life from a teacher-
centered to a student-centered philosophy also affected her at the core of her
being. She initiated a program focused on attacking burnout and rustout in her
personal life. Rustout, she realized, had also been eroding her marriage and
her relationship with her two children. When her husband refused to seek
counseling with her to put back the spark in their marriage, Amanda sought
counseling for herself. This support helped her to improve her self-esteem and
communications skills. Amanda also rewarded herself with a conscious pro-
gram of personal growth experiences. A regular program of exercise combined
with sensible eating helped her overcome years of yo-yo weight-loss/weight-
gain cycles. She rediscovered the joy of reading. She attended concerts and
public lectures. She found new delights in taking bit parts in community the-
ater. Most of all, Amanda's new perspective on life gave her a sense of per-
sonal and professional efficacy she had never experienced before. She was
learning how to make a real difference in her own life and in the lives of her
family, friends, and students.

CAUSES OF BURNOUT

We have described the processes of rustout and burnout as essentially resulting from excessive stress in the workplace, especially from the demands
placed on teachers. As we mentioned in the previous chapter, the teaching
profession is among the most stressful of all occupations because of the daily
unrelenting pressures and fragmented demands from a number of sources—
students, parents, and administrators as well as from the teacher's own high
expectations and hopes.

There are three main reason why teachers burnout. The first factor, *emo-*
tional exhaustion, is the logical consequence of overextending yourself—
trying to do too much or to keep up with a workload that is overwhelming.
The second factor, *depersonalization,* describes what takes place when
teachers develop negative attitudes toward others with whom they work.
They become cynical, frustrated, and critical. The third factor relates to a
perceived lack of personal accomplishment. Burned-out teachers feel *disil-*
lusioned because they are not satisfying their own needs for challenges, recognition, and appreciation. They feel discouraged about themselves because
their work does not provide them with sufficient feelings of fulfillment. In
addition, they feel isolated and misunderstood.

Beginning teachers may think themselves immune from such distressing
symptoms given their initial enthusiasm and excitement. However, almost

one-third of beginning teachers end up quitting the profession within the first few years, largely because their unrealistic expectations were not met and their impatience and competitiveness were not appropriately managed. They feel like they lost control—of their students, their environment, and mostly themselves.

In addition to these internal factors that predispose certain people to rustout or burnout, there are also a number of external factors that are part of the teacher's role of answering to so many different constituencies. For example, most schools are still hierarchically organized in such a way that they prevent teachers from collaborating together. Teachers spend most of the day in a room without any contact with other adults. Furthermore, a teacher's whole professional life is ruled by schedules, if not bells, signaling that it is time to move on to another activity whether you are ready to do so or not. And when teachers do get together for a meeting, they often focus primarily on announcements rather than interaction. One director of student teaching observed after supervising hundreds of beginning teachers, "How can we be reflective or work cooperatively with colleagues when our time is so filled by an imposed structure?"

Back to Difficult Students

"Teaching would be a great job . . . if only we didn't have to deal with students," one cynical teacher was heard to say. Indeed, one of the most common complaints made by teachers around the world is about those children who misbehave and are uncooperative—as we've mentioned, those who drive us crazy. These are the students, whether emotionally disturbed or simply ornery, whose primary mission in life it seems is to disrupt classroom proceedings and make the teacher's life as miserable as possible.

The comedian George Carlin, one of the most famous disruptive students of all time, freely admitted he got most of his training as an entertainer while attending parochial schools. What better place, he reasoned, to hone one's skills of making people laugh than in a setting where they are under such strict prohibitions not to do so? Carlin therefore perfected his routines of disrupting the class and infuriating the teacher through an ingenious assortment of obscene sounds, noises, and miscellaneous tricks. His favorite was "the pigeon," because he could make the sound deep in his throat, swallowing obnoxiously but unobtrusively, all the while looking around with everyone else trying to identify the culprit.

Carlin and other class clowns just like him are repeatedly asked by exasperated teachers, "Why do you do this? Why must you behave so atrociously?" The obvious reply, of course, is, "Because it is fun." Think back to your school days: It was such a delight to engage in forbidden activities, to break rules, to test yourself against authority figures, to make your friends laugh. During a time when you did not feel very much in control of your body or your life; when parents, teachers, and other grownups were always telling you what to do and how and when to do it, what exhilarating power you felt proving that you could get to one of them by making a teacher mad.

This is not all innocent fun. The class clown is more a source of minor annoyance (and sometimes even secret delight to the teacher with a sense of humor) than of serious stress and opposition. There are other children, however, whose disruptive behavior results not so much from harmless mischief as from some serious emotional disturbance. They are the children with major chips on their shoulders and axes to grind—especially with adults in positions of power over them. Many of them have been verbally and physically abused; others have been neglected or emotionally abandoned. Still others are just downright ornery, constitutionally obnoxious. They are hostile, seething with rage. They may be sociopathic, without conscience or moral responsibility. Others are just lost, aimless, nihilistically striking out at whoever is readily available. Many of them carry weapons and engage in fantasies of seeking violent revenge.

Regardless of the reasons why some children misbehave—whether they are crying out for help or just plain mean—they present a constant source of stress for teachers who must find ways to neutralize their inappropriate conduct. Discipline problems, after all, are the number one complaint by teachers as to what they dislike most about this work.

Peek into one "classroom from hell" where the teacher is trying to get through a lesson:

Teacher: Frieda, would you please stop whispering to Sasha and pay attention?

Frieda: I wasn't whispering to Sasha; she was whispering to me.

Sasha: I was not!

Frieda: Yes, you were!

Teacher: That's enough! Both of you . . . Hey, over there! I asked you boys to put those pictures away. You can look at them after school.

A voice: Go to hell, teacher! You can sit on my pictures.

Teacher: Who said that? I want to know right now who said that! [Silence for the first time that hour]

Teacher: Now, where were we?

A voice: Sitting on Mike's pictures.

Teacher: Felipe, I heard that. Are you saying that Mike was the one who yelled that out?

Mike: It wasn't me. [Aside to Felipe]: I'm going to kick your ass after school.

Teacher: Well, I don't think this is very funny. Sasha and Frieda, would you please stop whispering again?

Well, you get the picture—and hopefully it isn't *too* familiar.

A certain amount of resistance, if not defiance, is a normal part of a teacher's life. And that is why it is so critical that we learn to take this in stride and do what is in our power to take care of ourselves and keep our sense of humor intact.

Day after day, we are called upon to mediate petty skirmishes, break up fights and conflicts. Such incidents take their toll on the most tranquil educator, especially if steps are not taken to bring the students (and yourself) under control. That is why we become so desperate for new, foolproof discipline and intervention strategies, why we buy books like this one, or attend in-service workshops hoping for some kind of divine revelation. Yet what we learn over time is that almost all successful techniques are not magic wands but rather relational strategies that follow certain practices that utilize the following:

- Being carefully and sensitively vigilant to possible early cues of rule violations *before* they escalate to the point of disruptive behavior: *Meghan is getting antsy. Time to distract her before she starts acting out.*
- Establishing and enforcing rules and boundaries consistently: *Prakash has been a model student, but I can't let him get away with this.*
- Following through on disciplinary actions that include both rewards for constructive behavior and consequences for inappropriate behavior: *Kayla, I really appreciate you turning in your assignment on time.*
- Maintaining a mental state in which incidents are not overpersonalized: *This isn't about me.*
- Demonstrating a degree of emotional neutrality and situational objectivity: *Take a deep breath. This isn't a challenge to my authority but merely a way this student is seeking attention.*
- Focusing on the situation and the student behavior rather than labeling the person: *He isn't a difficult person but only behaving in challenging ways when he feels threatened.*
- Showing flexibility and adaptability since students have different needs and respond in different ways: *It's interesting how Karina actually becomes worse when I show her affection.*
- Owning some responsibility for conflicts since they usually are interpersonal struggles: *I wonder what I'm doing to activate this student or make things worse?*

It is often this last reminder that is the most difficult to remember, especially when in the throes of a difficult situation. It is so natural and easy to assign blame to students, especially because they are so astoundingly creative in the ways they act out. Yet it is a basic principle that within all interpersonal conflicts, both (or all) parties play a role in the struggle. One of the most useful and powerful ways to take care of ourselves is to acknowledge aspects of our own behavior that may need improvement; this is how we increase our personal and professional effectiveness.

Irate Parents

Second on the list of gripes among veteran teachers, after problem students, is difficult parents. What makes some parent conferences such dreaded events in the life of a teacher is the persistent, irrational, and misguided belief on the part of some people that their children are misunderstood, unappreciated, and unfairly treated. If only the teacher were more competent/intelligent/patient/skilled/experienced (choose one), then their child would not be having these problems. For those parents who do not want to accept responsibility for their children's academic or behavior problems, the easiest thing to do is to blame the teacher.

In its most civilized form, the parent hassle involves subjecting the teacher to subtle put-downs and insinuations of neglect or incompetence: "I suppose you are doing your best," or, "My son has never had these problems before he entered your class. I guess it must be a coincidence, huh?"

Some parents become belligerent, make threats, even act dramatically hostile in their accusations: "My daughter says you don't like her. That's why she doesn't do her homework or study for your dumb tests. I'm going to the principal to have you fired!" When the situation becomes heated or out of control, we do what we can to calm things down, or at the very least terminate contact before things become more abusive and disrespectful.

Some parents have had negative school experiences of their own (such as with learning problems, truancy, or failure) in the past. Perhaps they went to school in another country and are not familiar with American education or didn't even go to school. They may feel vulnerable or even threatened by teachers. Some are facing a host of problems in their lives. Both parents may work two jobs, take care of elderly family members, and take care of young children.

In most cases, parents are our greatest allies, whose support and encouragement make our jobs so much easier. During conferences, most parents only want to know what they can do to help their children and us in the educational process. They value our efforts and appreciate our dedication. Most of the time, if a parent does become unreasonable or disrespectful, an apology will quickly follow with the realization and acknowledgment: "I know you are doing the best you can. It's just that we have done all we can think of to try and motivate our daughter, and nothing seems to work. Now, we are expecting you to fix it all in a matter of months. You tell us what we can do to help."

All parents have dreams of their child becoming a neurosurgeon, trial attorney, professional athlete, corporate president, or U.S. senator. When evidence in the form of underachievement begins to show up, the parents' expectations are cracked, if not shattered. Parents want their children to have more than they had, to be more than they have been. You have felt these same pressures from your own parents throughout your life. Your disappointments become their failures. Your setbacks become their inadequacies. Because school performance is the primary measurement of childhood achievement in our society, each report card and parent-teacher conference is fraught with anxiety: "Is this the time when I will face the fact that my child is a loser?"

Once a teacher has been beaten up verbally by an irate parent, all future conferences may be dreaded as potentially explosive. This pressure is heaped on top of other kinds of interpersonal difficulties that are often part of the political-social organizations called schools.

Needless to say, meetings with parents can easily become emotionally charged. There is a tremendous amount at stake. Discussion must be handled very carefully and diplomatically by the teacher, acknowledging the stress for all parties concerned. The helping attitudes and behaviors described in Chapter 4 will be useful in your interactions with parents. An approach of enlisting parents as partners in the education and welfare of the children helps focus the conference into developing an action plan that will benefit all the stakeholders.

Collegial Backbiting

It is ironic that the teacher must contend with not only pressures from without—difficult students and parents, a public with little regard or respect for the profession—but also interpersonal strains from within the school. Some teachers report that they encounter little difficulty from students or their parents; the problems come from their own colleagues. One veteran teacher with fifteen years of experience describes this situation:

I love teaching. When I am in the classroom the whole world stops for me. I don't have a problem in the world. Most of the kids are great to work with and even the ones who are feisty eventually come around with a little patience, support, and firm limits. I rarely have problems with parents, either. They just like to be treated as partners and want a chance to be heard.

If I could just be left alone with my kids, everything would be wonderful. All of my stress comes from dealing with my colleagues, so I try to stay away from them. There are only a few people I will eat lunch with because those are the ones who aren't so threatened by new ideas and who genuinely like children. All that the other teachers do is talk about one another behind each other's backs and complain all the time. They complain about playground duty. They complain about the custodians. They complain about the heating, the parking, the administration, the union, their salaries. Most of all, however, they complain about the kids. I just try to stay out of their way and do my job.

Misery loves company and in some schools it abounds in the teacher's lounge as this teacher describes. Those who do not support "the cause" and do not speak in conformity with the others, will feel pressure from those who do.

A school is no different from any other human organization. We have a collection of well-educated, highly experienced people who are experts at imparting knowledge and skills to others. They are used to talking and having others pay close attention, even take notes on what they are saying. Each of these professionals has a healthy ego and strong opinions and wants to be respected by peers. What we have, then, is an enriched but enmeshed school environment. Coalitions and political factions are inevitable within school teams and departments and within the local teacher association. Administrators and school board members are often viewed with suspicion and distrust. All too frequently, the principals are seen less as benevolent supervisors and instructional leaders than as tyrants, authorities who get in the way of teachers doing their jobs with various mandates of their own or from the district office.

Despite what the disillusioned teacher said earlier in this section, teaching is the kind of job in which you need collegial support to survive, much less to flourish. It is imperative that you feel you belong to a group of peers who share your values and interests and, most of all, whom you can trust. Stress effects from other sources are magnified when your collegial relationships are less than supportive.

STRESS MANAGEMENT AND SELF-CARE STRATEGIES

Each of the sources of stress previously mentioned, although experienced by many educators, need not inevitably tear you down. You can prepare yourself with a number of strategies, such as those described next, that will serve you well in your efforts to stay calm, comfortable, and productive even in the face of very difficult circumstances.

Building a Support System

Probably the single most important thing that you can do to keep yourself energized and to prevent the rustout that stems from the sources of stress just mentioned is to create a support system that offers you nurturance, compassion, understanding, and direction when it is needed. Family and friends are, of course, important to help you diversify your relationships and provide support and acceptance. A surrogate family at work is just as important, made up of those colleagues whom you most trust. Early in your career, these colleagues will be important in showing you the routines of your school and in sharing with you all the do's and don'ts expected by the building principal, the other faculty members, and the parents at your school. Some teachers prefer to find colleagues to talk to from outside of their school and so make a special effort to attend as many district meetings and in-service programs as possible. It does not make much difference how you arrange your collegial support, as long as you do something constructive—such as develop a place in which you feel safe and accepted and understood.

For those teachers who enjoy or require even more intense and stimulating supportive experiences, there is also the option of joining a counseling or therapy group. This is not necessarily done because teachers perceive they have emotional problems; rather, they wish to find an environment that will help them to grow. In one such group designed specifically for teachers, a number of issues arose that have universal appeal:

- "Is what I'm doing with my life really all that worthwhile?"
- "How can I change the routines of my life so that they don't seem so repetitive and boring?"
- "Now that I'm settled into a career and a lifestyle, is this all there is?"
- "I am so good at being loving at work with the children. How come I have so much trouble finding a good relationship outside of work?"
- "What can I do to take care of the problem I am having with my spouse? Nothing I've tried so far seems to work."

These and similar personal and professional questions are considered during a teacher's normal reflective time. Regardless of the teacher's discipline, specialty, or institutional level, most teachers tend to be thoughtful and inquiring. We live a lifestyle that encourages us to consider difficult questions, to review consequences of our actions, to read and study, to make sense of the world, and to help others to do the same. This is sometimes lonely, very painful work. You will need lots of help along the way.

Learning to Relax

Relaxation involves letting go of all troubles and distractions. It means releasing all stress and strains in your life. Most of all, relaxation is a form of time-out, in which your body and mind are permitted to recuperate and rejuvenate themselves, especially after intense periods of work.

People relax in an endless number of ways—meditating, listening to music, watching television, driving in the car, walking, hiking, exercising, daydreaming, watching movies, soaking in a bath, playing with a computer, watching birds, or working on a hobby. The point is that these activities are not merely for entertainment, diversion, and leisure; they are necessary for you to function productively in other areas of your life.

As we've mentioned previously, it is absolutely imperative that ways be found to metabolize and dissipate the stress. If not, your rustout process will accelerate quickly or, perhaps even worse, you will resort to less healthy ways to deal with things. Alcohol and other substance abuse, overeating, and other self-destructive habits are often the result of people's attempts to medicate themselves for the stress they feel in their lives. The time to begin life-long relaxation patterns is right now. If you wait until you feel that you are in over your head, more drastic solutions will be needed to pull yourself out.

Relaxation really means taking time out for yourself. It involves doing something for a period of time that is just for you. You are able, at least temporarily, to put all other aspects of your life aside while you concentrate on a single activity that makes you feel good. Right this moment, think about the stress you feel in your life, the pressures you carry around. There are people who have certain expectations for you, expectations you can never (or choose not to) live up to. There are obligations, tasks, responsibilities, burdens that must be met. There are relationships in your life that are conflicted or unfulfilled. There may be financial or time pressures that you are living with.

Just imagine adding to all the existing strains in your personal life the additional challenge of an everyday teaching job. Furthermore, picture one particular class you have, with more than its fair share of problem kids who are belligerent or unresponsive to all your efforts. What will you do to keep yourself calm in the face of students' lack of progress, defiance, and opposition? How will you maintain your composure when the pressures pile on top of you?

The way in which you structure your life will determine, to a great extent, how well you will cope with unexpected bumps along the road. This includes such things as sleeping patterns, eating habits, ingestion of alcohol, even the pace at which you conduct your daily affairs. A teacher's lifestyle is an unusual one, structured as it is with working hours and vacations that are distinctly different from those of the business world. In fact, many professionals readily admit that the reason they chose teaching in the first place is that they liked the idea of getting home in the afternoon each day and having summers off. Yet, despite these windows of opportunity, this time off is often filled with additional burdens. For example, some teachers even find other jobs they can work during summers to supplement their incomes. The price they pay, of course, is sacrificing the qualitative longevity of their careers in exchange for meeting perceived economic needs.

One teacher explains, "Look, you think I like painting houses after school and during the summer? I don't do this because it's fun or I'm greedy or anything; my family needs this money to survive." When queried further as to what the extra money is used for, it becomes evident that its primary purpose is to provide for added luxuries—a boat, a sports car, a larger house that he would otherwise be unable to afford. This teacher is willing to give up his free time in order that his family may be more comfortable. Although this motive is laudable, when fall rolls around and the new school year is about to begin, he is already exhausted, whereas many of his colleagues return refreshed and eager.

A teacher with a lifestyle radically different from the previous one explains his philosophy:

> Sure, we would have more money, more things, if I supplemented our income with a part-time job. There are many things I wish I could afford. But I'm not willing to give up my precious time once I'm out of school. Since I work during prep periods during the school days, when the bell rings, I feel just like the kids: free! I like to spend this time with my family or puttering around the house. Because I get home before my wife, I'm in charge of cooking dinner, which I really enjoy. I finish up any grading or planning I might need to do after dinner. By the time school starts the next morning, I feel really rested.
>
> Summers are even more wonderful for me. I look at this time as 2 ½ months of uninterrupted indulgence, in that I can do whatever I want. I like to read novels, fix things around the house, go for long walks, sleep late. And then there is the travel . . . we usually take a lengthy family trip somewhere. Last summer, we spent a month camping and hiking in British Columbia.
>
> By the time school begins, I am usually restless and more than ready to get started. Ten weeks is a long time to be off with no structure. It really helps me to appreciate the daily routines of the school year.

Managing Time

There is such a variety of demands for your time that life as a teacher sometimes seems unmanageable. Taking charge of how you spend your time will give you a measure of control along with a sense of purpose and direction. Start by examining your values and then identifying your short-term and long-term, professional and personal goals. Determine what you feel is really important for you to accomplish, setting reasonable expectations and appropriate time lines. The next step is to create a specific list of things to do and strategize how you will accomplish your tasks. It's helpful to put it all in writing, including which people you need to contact and when, as well as what, if any, resources you will need in advance of an activity. Use a calendar to keep track of it all. In this way you can see where you have been, what you have achieved so far, where you are now, and where you are going. This will also provide a way for you to see how you spend your time.

One of my (Ellen) early mentors in my first school asked me every Friday what I was going to do for fun that weekend. Though I sometimes did work through the weekends the first month of that school year, this question did help me recognize I needed to balance my activities. I could see I wouldn't last the semester, much less the school year, unless I planned time for family and friends and some time just for myself, even if it was just reading a chapter of a novel. I began planning ahead and as time went on I would wait for her question with a ready answer.

At the same time, I had to explain to my family and friends that while my work day officially ended at 3:45 p.m., I still needed time at home in the evening and sometimes on the weekend to prepare for the next day. Plus, one night a week I was taking a graduate course for which I had to study and write papers as well. I separated myself from these activities when I was with them and let them know how much I appreciated their support. There were some times when I didn't want to be around anybody. I needed my "alone" time.

There are few other occupations that offer such a flexible lifestyle and so many opportunities for using your free time in fulfilling ways. But there is the danger of squandering this time or filling it with more burdens and obligations that take small pieces of your hide. There are many opportunities at schools to be involved—from committees to school clubs to after-school and evening programs for children and adults. The requests may seem to be endless. You can't do it all effectively all the time. Guard your schedule. For example, before a meeting or conference, even today I (Ellen) set an appointment with myself on my calendar to gather materials, such as grades or examples of student work; organize my thoughts; and, sometimes, generate an agenda. This way I can be prepared, present ideas clearly, and everyone's time will be used wisely.

It is up to you to structure your own life, plan your own time, teach others how to treat you, if you wish to reap the benefits of the teacher's lifestyle.

Training and Growth

Obviously the best way to deal with burnout and rustout is to avoid it in the first place. This means never allowing yourself to get to the point where your discouragement becomes intractable. Perhaps the best way teachers can stay fresh and energized is to have the courage and determination to keep making changes in what they do and how they do it. This includes, but is not limited to, the following:

- Request different teaching assignments every few years, with a different grade level or specialty area.
- Take a sabbatical to study and update your areas of expertise.
- Do a faculty exchange with a teacher from another community or country.
- Invite other professionals and resource people into your classroom to liven things up.
- Arrange team-teaching assignments with another staff member or university faculty member.
- Supervise a student teacher.
- Go back to school.
- Organize more field trips and out-of-class activities.
- Start a research project.
- Present at a conference.
- Apply for grants to study here and abroad.
- Integrate cutting-edge technology into your methods.

An elementary teacher relates:

Beginning my teaching career, I knew that my ultimate goal would be to find a way to reach more children than just those in my own classroom. My first year of teaching, I was too consumed with daily preparations, keeping up with parent communication, and learning how my team and school worked to be comfortable extending myself much beyond my own students. However, I noticed that there were a lot of changes going on in the school. Many colleagues were quick to make judgments and had many opinions, but few were serving on the advising committees with the principal.

My second year of teaching, I wanted to get involved. I wondered if I would be asked or if I would be welcome considering my relative inexperience. I had a close friend, a similarly young teacher, teaching at another school, who was very involved in administrative roles and had become well-respected at her school in a short amount of time. I asked her how she had been able to make an impact so quickly. She told me not to wait around for opportunities to come to me but to be proactive. This is similar advice for anything you want to achieve in life, but for some reason I was nervous to do this. I thought maybe you had to be really experienced and invited to serve on school committees. Gradually, I started talking to my principal more, attending extra meetings, and then I eventually asked to be on the advising committees to create a new report card and begin talks about curriculum change and mapping. Even though these committees were already formed, she gratefully accepted my request to be included. I have been able to represent my grade level as well as have my own opinions taken into consideration. Additionally, colleagues are now coming to me to ask questions, express concerns, or give ideas to take back to the committees or meetings with the principal. The extra time to be involved is significant, but I feel I am reaching more than just my own students now. I have become part of the process to make changes for students schoolwide.

Throughout our professional lives, people have often commented how "lucky" we are to have taught in so many different countries and contexts. We have received grants, sponsorships, or offers to study or teach throughout Asia, Africa, and South America, on Indian reservations and Aboriginal lands. Yet luck had little to do with these opportunities: We made tremendous financial and personal sacrifices in order to broaden our horizons and spice up the work. It is positively exhausting working in foreign cultures where language and customs are strange and challenging. We've repeatedly used up our savings to return to school, taken leaves, or quit jobs altogether in order to pursue new and stimulating opportunities. In many cases, we had to start over again after returning from an assignment. Yet feeling stale, bored, or burned out was the least of our concerns.

It is not that we are advocating radical solutions to keep yourself fresh— although it sure is exciting and fun—but rather that each of us has the capacity to reinvent ourselves if we are willing to invest the time, effort, and resources. There is no doubt that there is indeed a price to be paid for such professional or personal adventures.

When I (Jeffrey) was young, and even more impressionable, I met a woman while traveling who was riding her bike around the world (but I assume not across bodies of water). She was considerably older than me, a bit dowdy looking, and not at all what I imagined an adventurer would look like. She was traveling with a group of other cyclists, but because of her age and lack of athletic prowess, almost always finished hours after the rest of her team.

"Gee, you're so lucky to have this opportunity," I said to her with genuine envy in my voice. I was soon heading back to work after a week of spring break.

"Lucky? *Lucky?* What the hell does luck have to do with it?" All of a sudden, it was like a switch got turned on and she was absolutely furious.

"Ah," I backpedaled, "sorry about that. I didn't mean . . ."

"Hey, it's okay," she interrupted. "I'm sorry I jumped on you. It's just that I hear that so much from people. They think I'm rich or something, taking a year to travel around the world."

I cocked my head, as if to say that was my assumption as well.

The woman started to laugh. "Rich? Me? Do you know what I do for a living, or what I used to do?"

I just shook my head.

"I worked for the phone company for fifteen years, and even after all that time, I could barely make ends meet. But I sold my house. I sold everything I owned. And then I just took off to see the world. If I can do this, *anyone* can. It's just that people feel stuck in their lives and they're so afraid to take risks."

I was in awe of this woman. She was my hero. I never had any intention of quitting a job without a backup plan, but this stranger, someone I knew for only an hour of my life, inspired me to think about all the ways I could invigorate my life whenever I felt dissatisfied or trapped.

Any of us has the potential to change some aspect of our lives when things feel stale. Teachers complain so often to themselves, and one another, about how tired they are of the same old thing. Every time I hear that, the response inside my head (almost nobody wants to hear this out loud) is: So, why don't you do something about that?

There are so many good excuses for why it's not possible to change your assignment, switch jobs, make lifestyle changes, or learn something new. You can't afford it. You don't have time. This isn't the right time (but maybe later). You have too many other responsibilities. There are people who depend on you. There are others who won't let you make changes. You don't have any other options. You don't have the skills or resources. You don't know what you want to do. The list goes on and on. But what they all say is that you're not willing to do what it takes to revitalize your life because you don't want to pay the price or invest the time and energy. If that's the case, then at least accept that this is the way things are and make the best of it.

Finding meaning to your work, even the aggravation and stress you will occasionally be subjected to, is the key to preventing burnout. Being reflective about what you do and how you do it is the single most important commitment that teachers can make to keep themselves invigorated about their work. We'll discuss this topic at length in the next chapter.

ACTIVITIES AND APPLICATIONS

1. Flourishing as a teacher means, in part, diversifying your life and the sources of satisfaction you receive. Form or join a group that focuses on a common area of interest outside of school, such as a book club, movie night, morning runners/walkers, band, choir, or hobby-related gathering of people to strengthen connections with others and feel a sense of accomplishment outside of the classroom.

2. Analyze the behavior of those students who distract your and others' attention. There is so much written about the motives and consequences of such behavior, but what do *you* think are some of the main reasons why students act out? Which relational strategies will be most effective with your students?

3. Think of a time that you felt burned out in an activity or job that you had once loved. What were the causes of your loss of interest and commitment? If you had decided to remain in this situation (or perhaps are still there) what could you do to reenergize yourself?

4. One of the best predictors of remaining energized and passionately committed to a teaching career (or almost any career) is having a solid support system. What are some ways that you could proactively build more support in your life through collaboration, friendships, and other relationships?

10

Reflective Practice

What is it that you do best as a teacher? What are your signature strengths and resources that make you most effective in the class-room? What are some aspects of your style that could—and should—be improved? What do you struggle with the most in your work and in your life? What is your best understanding of what makes the greatest difference to your students in terms of inspiring them to learn? What is one thing you did with your last group of students that you'd like to do more frequently? What is one thing that you'd like to avoid in the future? These are just a few of the reflective questions that lead to excellence in any profession—that is, critically examining what it is that we do that is most and least helpful to others.

The teacher's journey is one that is punctuated with a series of required courses, workshops, in-service programs, and mandatory meetings, all designed for skill acquisition and technical knowledge. The last few decades of teacher preparation have been characterized by a prescriptive view of teaching, one that follows rules and procedures by formulae, and then measures progress through student testing. During this same period of time, many educational publishing companies developed so-called teacher-proof textbooks and instructional programs, which provide elaborate guidelines and scripts for use in classrooms. The idea is that teachers would not have to think, just follow the instructions provided.

What is often left out of the picture is that teachers are far more than technicians; we are called upon to improvise, trust our intuition, develop close relationships, and most important, to reflect critically on what we do and how we do it. This is easy to suggest but very difficult to implement because of the complexity of the process that demands a high level of commitment.

ON BEING A REFLECTIVE PERSON

Although we could debate for some time whether reflective people are born or made—in other words, whether some people are naturally inclined to be contemplative or people learn to be that way—we take the position that anyone, whether a teacher or a student, can become more reflective once the decision is made that this is an important goal and life priority. The first question to consider is whether being reflective is actually a desirable outcome for people in general, and for teachers in particular.

Being reflective essentially means being an independent thinker. It means knowing how to reason, to think for yourself, to combine intuition and logic in the process of solving problems. It means being introspective about phenomena that take place both within your internal world and in the world around you. This task, we believe, is among the most important missions of the teacher, for teaching involves so much more than presenting information, applying technical skills, or managing a group of children. It is a process by which people are taught to evaluate and process.

Assuming that you believe that among the best things that you can accomplish in your work is to help children become more reflective themselves, more like fearless truth seekers, constructive risk takers, and inquiring thinkers, then the best way (and certainly the most authentic and congruent means) to accomplish this goal is by modeling the values you consider to be most sacred.

Carnie, for example, is sometimes criticized by her colleagues and department head because she strays from mandated objectives. Her job is to teach art appreciation, and her directive is to encourage children to experiment with a number of artistic media. The problem, however, at least as it is labeled by her peers, is that she does not teach what she is supposed to teach. Any given class may find her wandering off course, provoking a discussion in the class about sexist and racial discrimination as they are manifested in art objects, or the impact of what is considered to be politically correct on artworks that have been commissioned throughout history.

Although Carnie sees herself as an art teacher, she considers herself to be, more than anything else, a stimulator of education that transcends disciplines. She wants her students to learn to love art; to value their own creative powers; and to understand that aesthetic efforts cannot be separated from political, historical, sociological, psychological, and literary movements of the time.

Carnie is a reflective professional because she considers that to be such an important priority for her own life. Although some of her colleagues may view her as "scattered," since she covers such vast subject matter, her students are captivated by her voracious appetite for knowledge and her intense desire to make sense of the world. They, too, have learned to become more reflective about the meaning of art in their lives and its place in the world of politics and commerce. Many of her students, even the very young ones, tend to begin their contributions in class with the preface, "I have been thinking about something that was said last time."

Children learn to be reflective when they can see for themselves that this is a valuable way to be. Even if it will not directly make them more money, win friends, and influence people, they will learn to find more peace within themselves and will develop more wisdom about the way the world works.

What It Means to Be Reflective

It should now be clear that becoming more reflective as a teacher depends very much on how you define yourself as a person and as a professional. These are some of the attributes of such an approach:

- *Asking why.* The reflective person is inquisitive. This trait can sometimes be irritating to others who resent the determination on the part of an individual who constantly questions the status quo: "Why does it have to be done this way?" "Why can't things be done differently?" Of course, the reflective person also tends to consider most vehemently those questions that are least likely to lead to single, right answers: "What is the meaning of life?" "What is my mission here on Earth?" "Why do people have to die?" "What happens after death?"
- *Finding patterns.* Being reflective means investing time and energy into trying to synthesize experiences, integrate knowledge, and bring together discrepant variables. It means being unrestricted by disciplines in the search for truth. The reflective person is constantly searching for the underlying reasons behind behavior and frameworks behind reality: "What makes people act the way they do?" "How do children learn and grow?" "What is the meaning of the collective silence in this classroom?"

The reflective person is intensely motivated to answer these and many other questions in the search for patterns of behavior and structures of the universe. In the truest sense of what it means to be a scholar, a Renaissance man or woman, the reflective person attempts to advance the state of knowledge by formulating innovative conceptions about what has been observed.

Both of these first two variables operative in the reflective person are found in Carnie. She listens to a talk by a well-known author about the disappointments in his life. She reads a biography of Van Gogh and notes the different ways that he struggled with failure in his life. She considers her own life and the ways in which she has fought for acceptance, first from her parents, then from her colleagues.

Suddenly, a lightbulb clicks on. An idea begins to take shape about the relationship between being disappointed and holding certain expectations for oneself and others. Carnie begins to delve into the literature in psychology but finds little on the subject. She starts reading novelists who deal with themes of failure—Dostoyevsky, Camus, Conrad, Plath. She reads biographies of famous people who struggle with disappointment—Galileo, Columbus, Freud, Dickens. Finally, her idea begins to take a more definitive shape, which she is able to articulate in a unifying hypothesis: There is a relationship between the amount of time someone spends anticipating a particular event and the subsequent disappointment the person feels if things do not work out as expected.

It is not this particular idea, its validity or merits, that is important. Rather, it is the *way* in which Carnie's mind works. She is constantly searching for answers, trying to understand complex issues by tying together contributions from diverse sources. Carnie is an art teacher, but she is so much more.

- *Reading voraciously.* As is evident from the example, reading widely broadens perspective. The reflective person, in order to make sense of things, must know about many different areas. It is not enough to be conversant in your discipline and professional identity; to be reflective, you must also be knowledgeable about world events, contemporary and historical societal trends, political and economic events, the arts, humanities, literature, and even current films, television and radio shows, plays, fiction, and popular websites. In short, the reflective person has taken the time to educate him- or herself about many different aspects of human existence.

- *Taking time for contemplation.* Solitude is a necessity for the reflective person. It is absolutely crucial to have structured time alone to recover from the demands placed on you by others, to consider where you are headed in your life, simply to make time for you to be able to reach deep inside yourself to find out what you think and feel about what is taking place around you. The reflective person structures private time as part of daily life, no matter what family or professional demands exist. Without the time and the opportunity to be reflective, even with all the talent and the best intentions, serious contemplation cannot take place.

- *Examining your own behavior.* The reflective person is a diligent student not only of world events and human behavior but also of his or her own actions. What good are wisdom and knowledge if you cannot apply them to your own life? Being reflective means considering the impact of your own behavior on others and accepting responsibility for the consequences of your actions. It means examining honestly what you are doing in your life and what effects (both positive and negative) you are having on others.

- *Confronting excuses.* Consistent with accepting responsibility for your actions is the belief that, with few exceptions, you are in charge of your own life. If things are not going the way you would like them to, rather than blaming others or making excuses, the reflective person prefers to take possession of the problem. Although giving up external reasons why things are not going according to plan is uncomfortable, as a reflective person, this also gives you a sense of personal power, of being in control of your own destiny.

José, an eighth-grade social studies teacher, is at first quite upset about the average ratings he received from his principal for classroom management. His first instinct is to make a number of excuses and to externalize the problem: "This isn't fair. The principal didn't take into consideration the larger class size she gave me this year. Besides, it's not my fault that some of my students can't keep on task for very long. Why does she seem to give me all the hyperactive kids?"

Whether these excuses are legitimate or not is beside the point (the brighter you are, the better excuses you will come up with for things not going your way). José realizes that whether his principal evaluated him fairly or not, the bottom line is (1) he does not like feeling upset about something he cannot change, and (2) he wants to improve his classroom management skills for his own professional growth. Upon reflection, José much prefers the idea that he is the one who messed up; that way, the power is within him to do something to change it. Rather than blaming the principal or himself, José decides to focus some of his attention on becoming more knowledgeable and proficient in motivating student involvement in learning history.

- *Defining your professional mission.* Being reflective means infusing your personal curiosity and truth-seeking values into your professional identity. To be a truly reflective person, you have to find a way to integrate the elements previously discussed into your style of teaching.

ON BECOMING A REFLECTIVE PROFESSIONAL

Personal reflection is a way of life, not just an interesting intellectual exercise. When you acquire and value the habits of personal reflection, your professional life will be enriched. In this section, we focus our attention on creating an image of ourselves as reflective teachers. To create this image, we must first expand our understanding of what being a reflective teacher involves and why it is so important. Supported by this understanding, you can begin to prepare yourself to grow into the image of the reflective teacher you wish to become: one who takes time to process experiences and use the resulting knowledge to make changes for the future. We illustrate this process through the stories of two dedicated teachers at different stages of their career.

Terry: "It's not the way I thought it would be."

I wanted to be a teacher for as long as I can remember. As a child, I used to play pretend games with my younger brothers and sisters; I was always the teacher and they were my students.

So, it was natural for me to identify education as a major at the beginning of my college experience. I was so fortified by my experiences as a student tutor and inspired by outstanding models of excellent elementary teachers that I was even prepared to weather the criticisms of my college classmates about entering a low-paying, low-esteemed profession. I was also determined to endure what my classmates called "the frivolity of education classes" in order to get my teaching certificate. I had been ready for a long time to teach my own class of first-grade students.

I paid special attention to my methods classes and tried to acquire as much knowledge and as many teaching strategies as I could. I felt confident that because I really cared about students, I could reach them, especially if I had good command of teaching methods.

After I graduated, I was employed to teach fourth-graders in an urban school district. Although I was disappointed in not receiving a first-grade assignment, I was happy that I got a job. Because I cared about kids of all ages, I thought I could be an effective fourth-grade teacher.

Something, however, was different; something was missing. My principal gave me a great evaluation for my classroom management abilities. The years of working with children in church activities and as a tutor had prepared me to be a good disciplinarian, and that was what he appeared to be mainly concerned about. However, a small segment of my students did not respond to me. I really cared about them. I tried everything I could think of to win them over, but they didn't seem to care. Most of these students were boys with short attention spans, hyperactivity, lack of motivation, low ability levels. You name it, they had it.

I was finally convinced that I couldn't do anything to help them with their problems. After all, I had to help seventeen other students who really cared about learning. Some of my fellow teachers experienced similar resistance from some of their students. We used to trade war stories in the faculty lounge: "These kids just don't care. They watch too much television. They don't come to school ready to learn." Consequently, when we felt we could not do any more for these students, we referred them for a special education evaluation.

Don't get me wrong—while they were in my class I still cared for them. I did not put any pressure on them to learn. Many of them were minority students, and I was especially nice to them. While my academic students were working on story problems in math that required higher-level thinking skills, I let my nonacademic students work in the back of the room practicing arithmetic and then doing whatever they wanted, as long as they kept quiet. Some drew pictures of spaceships in combat with alien invaders. Others put their own words to rap songs. Silly things like that. I really didn't mind what they did, as long as they did it without disturbing others. Some of the teachers in my school let their "nonacademics" take naps at their desks; I never let them do that.

Katherine: "I don't have any magic."

I have been an elementary teacher for twenty-three years. Twenty-three years is a *long* time, but I've enjoyed every minute of it. Well . . . most of them.

I've been encouraged to go into school administration, but I really am a teacher. I like working with students on a daily basis. I believe teaching begins and ends with students. I am truly proud of all my present and former students. They send me Christmas cards and invitations to their weddings years after they were students in my first-grade classroom.

My principal tells people that I was born with the ability to motivate students. He embarrasses me when he calls me a "classroom wizard" who casts the spell of lifelong learning on students. This makes some of my colleagues joke that I use some incantation or magic wand to motivate students to become eager about learning.

I don't have any magic. Furthermore, I really don't believe that I can motivate my students to learn. I do believe now, after thinking about it for many years, that motivation must come from inside my students. If I have a secret, it is that I talk frequently to each of my students. I get to know all about them, their hopes, their fears, what they dream about, and what kinds of pain they have known. I try to find the gifts in all my students; I try to build on their strengths. Knowing as much as I can about them and how *they* view their world helps me to think of ways to tap into their inner motivation.

I consciously try to avoid naming and listing their limitations. When I discover their strengths, I search for significant learning experiences with which I can help them to build on their strengths. I try to structure my classroom space to encourage their active involvement in real learning. When they are really involved, I can become invisible and let them direct their own powerful learning. Most of the time, my students take responsibility for their learning; this success builds their self-esteem.

I also believe that I must establish a context for learning in which my students are encouraged to mutually esteem one another. I give them regular opportunities to share their lives and their interests with one another. What keeps me coming back to my classroom year after year, in addition to the warm vibrations I get from my students, are the many new things I learn and try. My principal calls me an "omnivore," because he says I attend every workshop, seminar, and professional conference I can. These professional activities give me a great deal of food for thought about being a better teacher, about being a better learner. I believe my enthusiasm for learning gives me a lot of material for teaching. I know it gives me real credibility with my students. They know I am a lifelong learner because they see I'm eager to learn outside of class and inside of class as well. Also, let me say this, because it's true: I have learned so much from my students that has really enriched my life.

Reflections on the Stories

Both of these teachers were highly successful in their undergraduate teacher education courses. They both got excellent letters of recommendation from their cooperating teachers and university supervisors. Their principals commend them. In some ways, they can both be considered effective teachers. They know their children very well and care very much about them. They use a variety of teaching strategies and have good classroom management. They even use reflection as a source for improving their teaching. With all these crucial features in common, what are their essential differences?

Of course, there are many differences in the levels of experience, professional attitudes, and personal beliefs. Both Terry and Katherine spent a considerable amount of time each day thinking carefully about the many decisions they had to make about learning experiences, instructional materials, classroom arrangements, and methods of instruction.

They were very different in their practice of "critical reflection." Critical reflection is the other important dimension of what teachers must do when they think about their professional work. It is the kind of reflection that helps teachers understand and appreciate the moral, spiritual, aesthetic, and cultural dimensions of a teacher's responsibilities.

Review Terry's story and you will see that she lacked several essential understandings and appreciations. Although she told us over and over about the importance she placed on caring, she did place limits on her caring. Only those students she was able to reach without a struggle were the recipients of her attention. She gave up on those students she thought lacked motivation or had difficulty maintaining focus—students she labeled as mostly boys with short attention spans, hyperactivity, lack of motivation, and low ability levels. She did not reflect critically on her moral responsibility to become culturally sensitive to the needs of her minority students. Finally, she did not critically reflect on the aesthetic qualities of what these so-called nonacademic students accomplished. If she had carefully reflected on their drawings of spaceships in combat with alien invaders and their rap lyrics, she might have found a key to the motivation of real and durable learning experiences for these students. Unfortunately, Terry did what many other well-intentioned but nonreflective teachers do: She lowered her standards for these students and referred them to specialists.

Katherine, on the other hand, did not give up on any of her students. She considered, in a critical way, the level of development, the hopes, fears, aspirations, pains, and strengths of each of her students. She believed that it is her moral responsibility to structure her classroom and learning experiences to build on the strengths of each of her students. She consciously helped each one of her students to find the patterns of academic success needed to build a solid foundation for his or her own self-esteem. She also encouraged her students to support one another through a celebration of their individual and collective accomplishments.

Katherine also was aesthetically sensitive to the importance of continuing the wonder of learning new things. She learned many things from her students; she learned many things from her colleagues and the many workshops she attended. Katherine's reflective ability made her a special teacher, not just because she had the technical teaching and classroom management skills needed to do things right, but also because she possessed the moral, cultural, and aesthetic understandings needed to help all her students.

HOW FAILURE HELPS

Nobody embraces failure, yet its lessons are often far more instructive than those times when everything works seamlessly. This is especially the case for reflective teachers who use such opportunities to examine critically what they could do differently in the future.

Rather than disowning or denying the fear of failure, with its corresponding side effects, it might be useful to look at some of the benefits that failures bring. In fact, the very label of *failure* is a judgment with a very negative connotation. Yet failure is inevitable for any professional who takes risks, experiments with new ideas, and engages fully with the world.

There are actually a number of quite positive outcomes that can result from failure, depending on how you choose to deal with such situations:

- *Failure promotes reflection.* It is during times of disappointment that you take time out to figure out what went wrong. You consider the situation with some objectivity. You deconstruct the steps of what occurred. And ideally, you learn from the situation so that you can improve your performance next time.

- *Failure stimulates change.* When things don't work out as expected, you are required to make adjustments, to stretch yourself in new ways. The alternative—continuing to do what doesn't work—will only get you in deeper trouble.

- *Failure encourages flexibility.* When one thing doesn't work, it is time to try something else. Imagine, for example, that a child with whom you are having difficulty continually disrupts class with various antics that are not even very amusing to the other kids. This child is not your worst enemy; rather, the child is giving you clear feedback to which you are paying attention. You might not know yet what would work in this situation, but you sure know what will not work—and that is what you are already doing!

- *Failure improves frustration tolerance.* Failure can help you to be not only more flexible but also more forgiving of yourself and others. Quite simply, there are some situations you will never control and some kids with whom you will never develop good relationships. As frustrating as this might be, you can feel sorry for yourself and become dispirited about it, or you can learn to accept your own limitations.

- *Failure teaches humility.* Failure reminds you that you are human. You are fallible. You make mistakes and misjudgments. Every day. You can both learn from your errors and improve yourself based on this valuable feedback.

- *Failure provides useful information.* When you try something, there are two possible outcomes: It works or it doesn't work. Instead of treating unsuccessful results as failures, a very strong label with its own baggage, you can instead think of them as useful feedback. This attitude of embracing failure as valuable input allows you to look at what you're doing more critically and then to make changes according to what the situation calls for. Failure is nothing more or less than feedback on the impact of any action.

REFLECTION AS REGULAR PRACTICE

If you see the benefits of becoming more reflective in your life and work, you must develop a plan and follow it until technical and critical reflection is a central part of who you are. Although commitment to the practice is certainly an important first step, being reflective requires time and effort. It requires you to be alone to examine and appraise, collect and connect your thoughts as you review what has transpired over the course of the day. This often takes place during the commute from work—that is, if you turn off your radio and cell phone. Some teachers are able to stay in their room after school for thirty minutes after all the instructional materials have been put away, the classroom chores completed, and the next day's lessons planned. Others like to get away to a serene place at a park, at a library, at home, or in the woods. We know some teachers who have made special arrangements with their spouses and children to respect their request to be left uninterrupted in the office, bedroom, or some other private space at home.

Teachers implement reflective practice in all kinds of ways. While some prefer solitude to write in their journals, revise their lesson plans, or make notes to themselves about things they wish to do differently, others prefer dialogue and debriefing with trusted colleagues. This works particularly well when the focus is not on the problem itself (complaining about students or colleagues), but rather on your own behavior.

Some teachers find it valuable to keep their journal or a small notepad beside their bed. They find that those last moments before sleep may often suggest personal and professional brainstorms and creative ideas that are worth recording. When you begin to develop the habit of being reflective, through the process of the daily recording of your ideas, you will be more able to capitalize on those brief or extended moments that present themselves.

For example, Joe is a high school math teacher who has to make a twenty-minute commute to and from school each day. He turns off the radio and uses this time, which used to be freeway madness time, for reflection. He has not only found time for reflection, but he has also developed safe driving habits. He stays in the same lane and drives within the posted speed limits.

Jane is another teacher we know, who maintains that if regular reflection is good for her, it must be good for her students as well. She and her students spend the first ten minutes of their school day in reflective activities. They ponder societal problems; they examine personal dilemmas; they brainstorm solutions; they explore relationships; they write all of their reflections in their daily journal and use these journal reflections as a seedbed for debates, stories, and discussions. If you are convinced that you need to be more reflective but are having problems getting started, look for a colleague, such as Katherine, Jane, or Joe, who would be willing to serve as a reflective teacher mentor for you.

Finally, one of the most important aspects of reflective analysis is brutal honesty evaluating effectiveness. This means trying to be as clear and frank as possible about what you are doing—what is working, what is not working, what can be improved, and what you are doing to get in your own way.

Whether conducted individually, with a partner, or in a group, reflection gives you the opportunity to explore in detail the results of your decisions—what went well and why, as well as what needs improvement. Whether daily, weekly, or biweekly, it allows you to analyze past events, acknowledging your accomplishments related to the development of your teaching skills and the successes of your students. You can identify and learn from mistakes in order to change what you do in the future. You may try getting to know more about your students and building relationships with them, using a different teaching strategy, implementing different grouping patterns, observing master teachers address the same concept or skill, reading professional journal articles on the topic, or seeking additional guidance from others. It is precisely this reflection on the past that allows you to grow in the future.

ACTIVITIES AND APPLICATIONS

1. What does it mean to *you* to be a reflective teacher?

2. Think of a time recently in which it felt like you "failed" at something that was important to you. How could you reframe this so-called failure as simply instructive feedback that what you were doing wasn't working and it's time to try something else?

3. Learning often results from acknowledging mistakes in order to improve in the future. We have also mentioned the constructive value of failure in that it draws attention to areas in need of upgrading. Think of a time in your life in which you failed miserably and yet, ultimately, this disappointment led to significant growth and new opportunities.

4. Reflect on your signature strengths to define or update your professional mission.

11

Being Passionately Committed

> *When you ask students to describe their favorite teachers, they frequently identify those who are caring and respectful, sometimes mentioning that they are highly knowledgeable and professional. Yet more often than not, the one characteristic that students appreciate the most is passion! Regardless of whether the subject interests them or not, whether they are even high performing in that area, they absolutely love teachers who show enthusiasm and excitement for what they are teaching. It is this passion that is contagious.*

Passionately committed teachers are those who absolutely *love* what they do. They are constantly searching for more effective ways to reach their students, to master the content and methods of their craft. They feel a personal mission, even a magical quest, to walk through life devouring new experiences, learning as much as they can about the world, about others, about themselves—and helping others to do the same.

THRIVING IN THE PROFESSION

How is it that some teachers can remain in the profession, year after year, with all its challenges they face, and yet still appear so enthusiastic and excited about what they are doing? Whereas some of their colleagues just go through the motions, these extraordinary professionals actually get better and better over time. They find new ways to reinvent themselves and remain stimulated. Their "work" is a labor of love.

Who *are* these exemplary professionals who thrive and grow ever more effective over the years? Here are a few representative examples:

A special education teacher: I worked with an autistic child who was not talking at all. He would have tantrums because of the frustration of not being able to communicate, at least in a way that most people could understand. I introduced him to an alternative picture-exchange system that I'd heard about from a presentation I'd attended. The tantrums became less frequent as he was finally able to communicate and actually began vocalizing words. Eventually he was speaking in simple but complete sentences, first only to me, then later to his parents and peers. I can't tell you how incredible this was to witness and to play a role in his progress. This is what sustains me and keeps me going, this feeling that I'm making a difference, especially with children who would otherwise not have a chance.

A reading teacher: The part about my job that I love the most is working with small groups to help students improve their comprehension. Most of my kids are struggling in the regular classroom and feel like they're stupid. My job is to help them get closer to their grade-level standards: This is my calling! I just love seeing the looks on their faces when they begin to decode words on their own and read a book by themselves. It's incredible how quickly their confidence improves and how I can help them succeed—not just in reading but in their other subjects as well.

A physical education teacher: My health curriculum included units on stress reduction, anatomy of the respiratory and circulatory systems, tobacco-use prevention, nutrition, and the importance of exercise. It's challenging to develop lessons that use all the students' senses and make the learning fun and relevant to their lives. Former students frequently come back to me and tell me how they remember some of the things I taught them about keeping themselves healthy by the lifestyle choices they make.

A middle school math teacher: I had a double block seventh-grade math class designed for "basic"- and "below basic"–designated students. My first day of school, I learned the name of a boy in my class: Oscar. He immediately sat in the back with a group of boys and by the end of the period he had managed to ask to go to the bathroom, to the nurse, and to get a drink of water. Throughout that first week, he had changed seats no less than five times. I looked in his cumulative file and found out that he had been in Honors Math and had scored at the advanced proficiency level on the standards test the previous year. I was stunned! How could a student so smart behave this badly? He was bored. I arranged for him to be transferred into an Honors Pre-Algebra class, pulled him aside, and told him the news. The look on his face was one that I will never forget. He tried to pull himself together and "act cool," but I knew that he was pleased. About a month after he left my class, he came back to visit me and say hello. He was a much different student than the one I had seen in my classroom. He complained that his math class was too hard, but I could tell that he appreciated the challenge. It felt great to know that I advocated on behalf of someone who felt trapped in a system that wasn't working for him and who didn't feel he had a voice to change it.

A high school science teacher: It's the field trips I love the most because I get to see the students actually involved in science in a meaningful way. Once they get out of the classroom, they appreciate so much more the way that science can help them make sense of things that puzzle them. Once we return to the classroom, they have so much to talk about; even the quiet ones seem to get excited. Hearing them use the language of science motivates me to incorporate more field trips in the future.

It's interesting what these stories have in common. A theme that seems to run throughout each of these narratives is that the teachers get so passionate and excited knowing that they have made a difference. They can actually see, if not measure, progress among their students. They seem to have a clear idea of what they do in their classrooms that is most impactful and influential, as well as most appreciated by their students. The teachers feel a sense of empowerment and efficacy because they see a direct correlation between their own efforts and the outcomes that result. They continue to grow over time, along with their students, because they are able to build on past successes, improving their practice.

Keep the Flame Burning

We hope a lot of this seems familiar to you. If you are already a passionately committed veteran teacher, we hope our book validates the daily effort you make to maintain your personal and professional growth—despite the discouragement and challenges you see around you. If you are preparing to be a teacher, we hope you hold on to the enthusiasm and passion that brought you into the field in the first place. That may seem easy, given your initial commitment, but the real difficulty is keeping that excitement going throughout your career. This is not only a challenge for teachers but for *anyone* who has worked in a profession for more than a few years. After all, how many people do you know who absolutely *love* their jobs?

There are certain practices that are most associated with teachers who sustain their passion and commitment over the years. We present these activities as samples of the ways that are mentioned most frequently by veterans who have been successful at keeping the flame of their passion not only alive but also burning brightly. Hopefully, many of them are already familiar to you, if not already part of your daily practice.

Take Care of Yourself

We have repeatedly focused on the inseparable linkage between the personal and the professional dimensions of being a teacher. We believe that a satisfied, fully functioning professional must first be a satisfied, well-adjusted person. Your first responsibility, as a person and professional, is to yourself. This is not selfish, narcissistic "me-ism" that we advocate, but a healthy regard for your own well-being and functioning. Students learn not just from what you teach in the classroom, what you tell them, but also the ways you live your life.

Regardless of your stage of professional development, each of us needs to be stimulated and encouraged by colleagues we trust and have our best interest in mind. Beginning teachers will find this essential for their survival, but experienced teachers, as well, need ongoing support and help throughout their careers. Teachers who work in isolation are far more susceptible to burnout and discouragement. Ideally, you would find someone who is not only knowledgeable but is also caring and approachable. You need support from those who are open and available to you, rather than feeling like you are a burden. Find colleagues who will support your interests and causes and whose projects you would like to join.

Make Learning More Meaningful

The best teachers you ever had were not merely those who were smart or who knew a lot; they found myriad ways to make their subjects relevant to your life. Mathematics, science, world languages, music, geography, English—no subject will be readily accessible to students unless you can create the means by which they can feel motivated to learn it.

You can, however, spend as much time and energy helping students to understand why they are studying a particular subject and how it will benefit them in their daily lives as you do any other aspect of the learning process. The best teachers are those who have infused their students with the passionate desire to learn what they have to offer. Period.

Be Interested and Interesting

Remember those few exemplary teachers who inspired you with their many and varied personal and professional qualities? If you looked at them more closely, you would recognize two common traits—they were both incredibly interested in you and were interesting people. Their passion for lifelong learning fueled their pursuit of new knowledge, new experiences, new opportunities to learn, and meeting new people. They were risk takers. They brought the world into the classroom for you to explore, examine, and question. They did not have all the answers and were not afraid to let you know that they, like you, were still searching. Their talent was for infecting you with natural curiosity to ask questions and find your own solutions. Because they were interested and interesting people, they had the knack of making education entertaining, and entertainment educational.

You too can seek out new experiences and share them with your students. Let them know what catches your attention; what you are reading; what projects you find meaningful, relaxing, engaging; how someone you met influenced your life; what you have learned. Find out more about your students. What do they know? What can they teach you and their classmates?

Instill Your Teaching With Greater Creativity

One of the reasons why any job becomes stale is because you tend to do the same things the same way, over and over again. Once you have planned a set of lessons plans with a collection of favorite activities, examples, and stories, it's challenging to push yourself to keep changing what you do and how you do it. It takes considerable work and effort.

As a teacher, you are likely to be more effective in making learning relevant if you infuse your instruction and classroom environment with ongoing creativity. You do not have to be a Picasso to enliven your classroom with art. You do not have to be a Mozart to use music to promote lively student responses. As a teacher, you decide what media (high tech or low tech) or multimedia to select to reach your intended outcomes with students. New tools and resources are developed all the time by other educators for you to try. Better yet, generate your own.

Balance Caring and Controlling

You can probably remember some caring teachers whose classrooms were pits of disorder. On the other extreme, you may also have experienced controlling tyrants who displayed little caring for students. When challenges overwhelm us, we have a tendency to try to control our environment. As a passionately committed teacher, you will work to balance these two important dimensions of teaching. Caring and controlling are not conflicting opposites; they are mutually supportive. It is the teacher's responsibility to work with students to establish the classroom boundaries that will promote self-discipline and encourage teachers and students to respect and care for one another. Your mission as an educator is not just to produce children who know things but to grow children who can think for themselves, who can solve problems ingeniously, who can make good choices for themselves, who can take our current base of knowledge and move beyond it as in the teachers' examples above.

Cultivate Your Deep Cultural Sensitivity

In North America, as in most of the world, nations are becoming more and more culturally diverse. We are composed of many subcultures with citizens who have the freedom to express their ideas, beliefs, and lifestyles. Ignorance and fear frequently prevent us from appreciating the variety of cultural traits and beliefs of other people. It is a part of the passionately committed teacher's moral responsibility to cultivate knowledge and appreciation of cultural diversity and to teach others to do the same.

Unfortunately, so many efforts related to cultural sensitivity are embedded in political correctness and token gestures that have little lasting impact. It takes real passion to be culturally responsive; to transcend the minimal efforts that are often part of school district policies; and to deal with real issues of racism, prejudice, and social justice. Once again, this involves far more than mere talk and attending a few in-service workshops; it means practicing in your life the sort of commitment to diversity and multicultural education that you hope for your students to have.

As a culturally responsive teacher, you strive to take action to support and advocate for your students. You campaign for high expectations of all students, multicultural resources, curriculum changes, more technology, longer library hours, additional advanced courses, increased classroom and school maintenance. You hold workshops for parents in the evening and on the weekends on child development and parenting, transitioning to middle school, college readiness, and other topics depending on the age of the students and needs of the community. You respect students' languages and their cultures, involve students in their learning, focus on their personal experiences, and facilitate development of their leadership skills.

Advance Your Own Education

We are not talking here about only the mandatory in-service programs that are often required by the school or district, but rather on what you choose to foster in your own knowledge and skills. There once was a time in human history, just a few hundred years ago, when what you learned during apprentice years served you well throughout your lifetime. The only "technology" was perhaps a firearm, and the main form of transportation was a horse. For those old enough to remember, it was just a few decades ago when the only technology a teacher had to master was changing the ribbon on a typewriter or threading a film on a projector. Nowadays, every five years seem to bring a revolution in technological breakthroughs, communication devices, and teaching resources. New developments in research every year routinely challenge some of our most sacred beliefs about learning and how it best occurs.

Most of us entered this field in the first place because we love learning. We not only so enjoy and feel satisfied by others' growth and development, but we also thrive on our own. We are hungry for new stimulation, new ways to define ourselves and structure what we do.

Besides this intrinsic attraction to learning, many teachers aspire to other positions in the education setting that allow them to put their accumulated years of experience to work in different ways. Some teachers complete master's degrees in their teaching area or related fields, such as reading or educational technology. Some expand their roles by seeking training and programs to work with student teachers or mentor new teachers. Others obtain additional degrees and leave the classroom to work in administration, curriculum, or school counseling. Additional education will meet your needs for intellectual stimulation. You'll also meet like-minded people, forming new relationships and expanding your horizons.

For those looking for a different avenue, membership in educational associations and professional organizations will help you sustain your idealism. National councils of teachers are organized by discipline, and they typically function on the local and state level as well. By attending annual conferences and local meetings of these groups you will mingle with other passionately dedicated teachers; keep on the cutting edge of pedagogical knowledge, practice, and research; and hear inspiring speakers. Many of these professional organizations publish outstanding journals, with articles and educational materials useful to classroom teachers, and host websites with a variety of teacher resources. They also offer opportunities for you to serve as officers, writers, editors, or other leadership positions.

Learn From Your Students

With knowledge increasing so quickly, we can hardly be expected to have all the answers anymore. Our students are inquisitive—and many are far more skilled at accessing information and sharing what they have learned than we are.

In so many ways, our students are our own best teachers. They give us clear, immediate, and consistent feedback about what works for them, and what doesn't—if we are paying attention. They teach us about their worlds, about their lives, and about their aspirations. In so many ways, they teach us about ourselves, our own lost dreams, our own fears and limitations. Among the most painful aspects of our work are the times when we have to relive our past failures and disappointments vicariously through certain students who are struggling. We see parts of ourselves in them, for better or worse, and the wounds we experienced begin to ache all over again. On the other hand, our students remind us about our own resilience, about what we have been able to overcome through force of will.

There is such an interesting process of reciprocal influence that occurs in our work—all the while we are teaching students, they are also instructing us on life lessons. The following two examples illustrate this point.

- Bring to mind a recent instance in which a particular student (or class session) had a significant impact on you personally.
- Think of the last time that you brought a personal experience into your teaching as a way to demonstrate a point.

In other words, who we are as human beings informs the way we operate as teachers. Likewise, all that we learn in our professional roles helps us to become more engaged, wise, and compassionate people. Everything we learn in our daily lives—every book we read, every film we see, every conversation we have, and especially every workshop, lecture, and class we attend—helps us to become more worldly and wise as well as expands our repertoire, bringing learning to life in the classroom.

Operating at our best isn't only when a class ends and we *know* we have reached some students or put together an almost flawless and exciting session. There are also those special times when we have learned as much as our students as a result of what transpired. This could be something as simple as a student question that stimulated us to think in new ways, or it could be something far more personal and profound in which our whole world was rocked by something that transpired during an interaction. If you think about it, *really* think about it, we are not only permitted to work on ourselves as a primary mission, but it is virtually a mandate as part of the teacher's journey.

ONWARD

There is no closure to this book. Your journey continues as you select from paths that open to you as you continue to be a caring, knowledgeable, and respectful teacher. This is the work of a lifetime. Teaching is a highly stimulating and rewarding profession. We hope we have motivated you to become a committed, passionate educator willing to pursue the relationship skills you need to be an effective teacher and an effective human being. May you continue to inspire and be inspired!

ACTIVITIES AND APPLICATIONS

1. What are some ways that you could more actively surround yourself with like-minded people who are passionate about what they do? Who are some of the teachers you admire the most, and what can you do to spend more time with them?

2. What do you think are the main differences between teachers who just go through the motions, content with a level of mere competence or even mediocrity, versus those who maintain their passion and are committed to excellence?

3. One of the ways that teachers maintain their enthusiasm and continued growth is by continually reinventing themselves, changing what they do and how they do it. Think of an area of your life right now in which you feel a little stuck and bored. What could you do to enliven that experience by thinking or acting more creatively?

4. Become an expert on what matters most to students and ex-students. Interview an assortment of people about what they appreciated most about their teachers. Ask them to look back on their experiences and talk about what mattered most.

References

Aultman, L. P., Williams-Johnson, M. R., & Schutz, P. A. (2009). Boundary dilemmas in teacher-student relationships: Struggling with the "the line." *Teaching and Teacher Education, 25,* 636–646.

Banks, J. A. (2009). *Teaching strategies for ethnic studies* (8th ed.). Boston, MA: Allyn & Bacon.

Barr, J. J. (2011). The relationship between teachers' empathy and perceptions of school culture. *Educational Studies, 37*(3), 365–369.

Cleaver, E. (1968). *Soul on ice.* New York, NY: Dell.

Conroy, P. (1982). *The Lords of Discipline.* New York, NY: Bantam.

Farber, K. (2010). *Why great teachers quit: And how we might stop the exodus.* Thousand Oaks, CA: Corwin.

Gentry, M., Steenbergen-Hu, S., & Choi, B. (2011). Student-identified exemplary teachers: Insights from talented teachers. *Gifted Child Quarterly, 55*(2), 111–125.

Gmelch, W. H. (1983). Stress for success: How to optimize your performance. *Theory Into Practice, 22*(1), 7–14.

Jesild, A. T. (1955). *When teachers face themselves.* New York, NY: Teachers College Press.

Kirschenbaum, H. (2007). *The life and work of Carl Rogers.* Ross-on-Wye, UK: PCCS Books.

Klassen, R. M., & Chiu, M. M. (2010). Effects on teachers' self-efficacy and job satisfaction: Teacher gender, years of experience, and job stress. *Journal of Educational Psychology, 102*(3), 741–756.

Kohl, H. (2008). *The Herb Kohl reader.* New York, NY: The New Press.

Kottler, J. A. (2008). *A basic primer of helping skills.* Thousand Oaks, CA: Sage.

Kottler, J. A., & Chen, D. (2012). *Stress management and prevention: Applications to daily life* (2nd ed.). New York, NY: Routledge.

Kottler, J. A., & Kottler, E. (2007). *Counseling skills for teachers* (2nd ed.). Thousand Oaks, CA: Corwin.

Kottler, J. A., & Kottler, E. (2008). *Students who drive you crazy: Succeeding with resistant, unmotivated, and otherwise difficult young people* (2nd ed.). Thousand Oaks, CA: Corwin.

Kottler, J. A., Zehm, S. J., & Kottler, E. (2005). *On being a teacher: The human dimension* (3rd ed.). Thousand Oaks, CA: Corwin.

Kozol, J. (2007). *Letters to a young teacher.* New York, NY: Random House.

Maslach, C. (1982). *Burnout: The cost of caring.* Englewood Cliffs, NJ: Prentice Hall.

Mead, M. (1927). The need for teaching anthropology in normal schools and teachers' colleges. *School and Society, 26*, 466.

Moll, L. C., Amanti, C., Neff, D., & Gonzalez, N. (1992). Funds of knowledge for teaching: Using a qualitative approach to connect homes and classrooms. *Theory Into Practice, 31*(2), 172–195.

Monroe, S. S. (1992). *Margaret Mead: Anthropological perspective on educational change* (ERIC report no. ED356168). Available at www.eric.ed.gov

Nieto, S. (2009). From surviving to thriving. *Educational Leadership, 66*(5), 8–13.

Nieto, S. (2010/2011). Humility in the age of hubris. *Educational Leadership, 68*(4), 74.

Palmer, P. J. (2007). *The courage to teach: Exploring the inner landscape of a teacher's life, 10th anniversary edition.* San Francisco, CA: Jossey-Bass.

Riley, P. (2011). *Attachment theory and the teacher-student relationship.* New York, NY: Routledge.

Rogers, C. R. (1969). *Freedom to learn.* Columbus, OH: Charles C. Merrill.

Rothstein-Fisch, C., & Trumbell, E. (2008). *Managing diverse classrooms: How to build on students' cultural strengths.* Alexandria, VA: ASCD.

Skovoholt, T., & Trotter-Mathison, M. J. (2011). *The resilient practitioner: Burnout prevention and self-care strategies for counselors, therapists, teachers, and health professionals* (2nd ed.). New York, NY: Routledge.

Spindler, G., & Spindler, L. (1994). *Pathways to cultural awareness.* Thousand Oaks: CA: Corwin.

Timm, J. T. (1996). *Four perspectives in multicultural education.* Belmont, CA: Wadsworth.

Tomlinson, C. A. (2010/2011). Notes from an accidental teacher. *Educational Leadership, 68*(4), 22–26.

Vanslyke-Briggs, K. (2010). *Nurturing teacher: Managing the stress of caring.* Lanham, MD: Rowman & Littlefield.

Index

CORWIN
A SAGE Company

The Corwin logo—a raven striding across an open book—represents the union of courage and learning. Corwin is committed to improving education for all learners by publishing books and other professional development resources for those serving the field of PreK–12 education. By providing practical, hands-on materials, Corwin continues to carry out the promise of its motto: **"Helping Educators Do Their Work Better."**